COACHING PERSPECTIVES IV

Center for Coaching Certification

Cathy Liska
Bill Peace
Tiffany Kalinka
Pamela Howard
Patti Oskvarek
Mikayla Phan
Danielle Hark
Karen Wrolson
Robbie Johnson
Dina Simon
Laura Posada
Bill Shell
Evette Beckett-Tuggle
Patricia Hughes

Copyright © 2014 by the Center for Coaching Certification LLC

All rights reserved. No part of this publication may be reproduced, distributed, or transmitted in any form or by any means, including photocopying, recording, or other electronic or mechanical methods without the prior written permission of the publisher, except in the case of brief quotations embodied in critical reviews and certain other noncommercial uses permitted by copyright law. For permission requests, write to 5072 Coral Reef Drive, Johns Island, SC 29455.

Full rights to the individual chapters in this book are granted to the respective author for their use, and they may grant rights to their individual chapters as they deem appropriate.

Names and identifying details have been changed to protect the privacy of individuals.

The authors and publisher have made every effort to ensure accuracy and completeness of the information in this book. We assume no responsibility for errors, inaccuracies, omissions, or any inconsistencies herein. Any slights of people, places, or organizations are unintentional. Although the authors and publisher have made every effort to ensure that the information in this book was correct at press time, the authors and publisher do not assume and hereby disclaim any liability to any party for any loss, damage, or disruption, either direct or indirect, caused by errors or omissions, whether such errors or omissions result from negligence, accident, or any other cause.

The information in this book is meant to supplement, not replace, proper coaching training. Like any profession, coaching requires training.

Dear Reader,

The training and writing journey with the Certified Professional and Master Coaches authoring chapters here has been a privilege. It is an honor to publish the fourth annual Coaching Perspectives book highlighting their expertise.

The content of these pages is helpful to individuals, to coaches, and to all involved with coaching. The combination of such diverse ideas is insightful for understanding the scope of coaching opportunities.

Each coach/author provides unique insights and expertise. Enjoy the reading, the new learning, and the immediately applicable concepts, techniques, and processes shared.

Kindly let us know how we can be helpful.

Sincerely,

Cathy Liska
Guide from the Side®
Center for Coaching Certification

CENTER FOR COACHING CERTIFICATION

www.CenterforCoachingCertification.com

Info@CenterforCoachingCertification.com

800-350-1678

MISSION:

Enhance your coach training experience with quality, professionalism, and support.

VISION:

A high-quality, ethical norm throughout the coaching industry achieved through leadership by example.

*For coaches,
those thinking about becoming a coach,
and those who receive coaching.*

Table of Contents

Creating a Coaching Culture *by Cathy Liska*……………………..1

Your Office as Coaching Central *by Bill Peace*……………...….…27

Client-Centered Coaching *by Tiffany Kalinka*……………….…...50

Creating Your Personal Strategic Plan *by Pamela Howard*……...69

Coaching for Leadership *by Patti Osvarek*……………………......86

Attention Deficit or Attention Different? *by Mikayla Phan*….....108

Coaching Thru Mental Health Challenges *by Danielle Hark*…..129

Coaching Parents with Teens *by Karen Wrolson*……………......148

Benefits of Coaching All Generations *by Robbie Johnson*….…..172

Career and Transition Coaching *by Dina Simon*……….............192

Clap for Change *by Laura Posada*……………………….…...…..210

Three Secrets to Selecting a Coach *by Bill Shell*…….................233

The Phenomenal Coach *by Evette Beckett-Tuggle*……….….......253

The Structured Discernment Process *by Patricia Hughes*………275

CREATING A COACHING CULTURE
Cathy Liska

COACHING AND A COACHING CULTURE

As of this writing, coaching remains widely misunderstood. Some think of sports coaching where the coach is telling the athletes what to do and driving them forward. Additionally, the terms mentor and consultant are often mistakenly used interchangeably with the term coach. In the workplace, Human Resource and training professionals are often seen as coaches – sometimes they are also trained as coaches and sometimes they themselves misunderstand the differences.

> *"Other professionals give advice*
> *and a coach asks questions."*

Coaching is completely different than the other professional roles.

What is the difference between other professional roles and coaching?
- Other professionals do the talking and a coach listens.
- Other professionals give advice and a coach asks questions.
- Other professionals focus the conversation on their own experience and a coach focuses the conversation on enhancing the skills and outcomes for the other person.

- Other professionals serve to share expertise and are essentially teachers while coaches serve to develop expertise and are more similar to facilitators.
- Other professional roles are the expert with the answers and a coach is the expert at eliciting the answers from the person doing the work.

Each of the approaches provides value. Other professionals add value by sharing experiences, expertise, and advice. Coaching adds value by engaging people to explore their options, expand their thinking, develop their action plans, and follow through.

For example, responses to this statement will vary: "A co-worker lied to my boss about what happened and made me look like an idiot!"

- Friend: "Wow, you must be so mad at them!"
- Consultant: "Let me analyze what is happening and give you a plan."
- Mentor: "You should confront the co-worker and explain it to your boss."
- Coach: "What outcome do you want to work towards now?"

The value of the friend is having someone understand and support. The value of the consultant is their experience and expertise. The value of the mentor is their wisdom. The value of the coach is they empower you to think it through and make intentional choices about your actions.

The International Coach Federation (ICF) defines coaching as "a strategic partnership in which the coach empowers the client to clarify goals, create action plans, move past obstacles, and achieve what the client chooses." The ICF publishes a table that explains how coaching competencies are evaluated with reasons credentialing may be denied. Here is one measurement: "For example, if a coach almost exclusively gives advice or indicates that a particular answer chosen by the coach is what the client should do, trust and intimacy, coaching presence, powerful questioning, creating awareness, and client generated actions and accountability will not be present and a credential at any level would be denied."

Bottom line, if someone is telling, directing, or advising, they are NOT coaching. Instead coaching involves listening and asking questions.

Developing a coaching culture and using a coaching style of management with listening and asking questions is increasingly a tool used in organizational development. On a personal level, coaching skills help with relationships at home, with friends, and in the community.

Pros of a Coaching Culture:
- Perceived as positive and appropriate at all levels
- Proven impact on skill development and results
- Increases engagement and motivates productivity

Coaching empowers people to find and apply their own answers. It is positive. It is proactive. It works.

> *"Coaching enhances outcomes because people value the experience of others seeking to understand them and acting on their ideas."*

BENEFITS OF A COACHING CULTURE

Remember the decision maker (parent, community leader, or boss) saying, "my way or the highway" as the standard? Then it shifted to, "I'll say what I think and you tell me why you like it." The norm now is offering advice or solutions. These approaches fail to fully engage or motivate long-term results. In a coaching culture differences are recognized. Each person is valued for their strengths and yes, weaknesses. A coaching culture creates awareness about how different people think, decide, and act, and how to work with them effectively based on who they are and their preferences.

Coaching enhances outcomes because people value the experience of others seeking to understand them and acting on their ideas. Individuals want to feel that they are important. A coaching leader is a strategic partner that:
- Asks questions for the clarifying of goals
- Explores options for moving past obstacles
- Empowers the creation of action plans

- Supports discovery of opportunities to achieve
- Empowers decision making and action

How? A coaching leader takes time to ask about goals and actions for moving forward. The individual is empowered to think about overcoming obstacles and create their own plans so they are engaged and follow-through increases exponentially. The coaching leader delegates responsibility effectively and supports individual growth. The coaching leader encourages individual decision making and action. Plus, the coaching leader verbally acknowledges contributions so individuals are aware of being valued and valuable.

A coaching culture focuses forward. Rather than talking about what happened, who did it, or who said it, ask: Where are we now? Where do we want to be? How do we get there? How do we prevent this problem in the future? This coaching approach engages people in finding solutions and creating results.

> "...coaching approach engages people in finding solutions and creating results."

CREATING A COACHING CULTURE AT WORK, HOME, AND IN THE COMMUNITY

Whether managing people, parenting, volunteering, or participating in community events, coaching skills make leadership easier. True leadership is about empowering others and enhancing their innate skills. While it is easy to give advice and suggestions, an individual figuring out their own answer is more effective.

In the workplace talent retention, employee engagement, productivity, and goal achievement are driven by the effectiveness of the leaders. Developing leadership competency in an organization calls for coaching skills training. Coaching skills support team building and spread throughout the organization, ensuring the talent and processes are in place for long-term organizational success.

Coaching helps with change. Imagine an office is going through a change in personnel that results in re-assigning duties and re-arranging work space. Without coaching skills each person focuses on telling and advocating for their ideas. With coaching skills, everyone discusses what is significant in determining work assignments and work space. In a team meeting, through questioning and sharing perspective, a coaching group explores options. Ultimately a consensus is reached so each person buys-in to the outcome. The coaching skills of understanding, asking questions, and exploring support a productive outcome.

Coaching helps deal with angry customers. Imagine someone is angry about a purchase and is vocal and disruptive. Without coaching skills the employee explains the policy regarding the warranty and returns. With coaching skills the employee asks the customer about their experience and what they want; if the customer wants something that is undoable, the employee asks for other possibilities. If the customer is stuck on an unreasonable option, the employee says, "Given that I am unable to do this, what I can do is give options and let you choose what works for you now." After providing multiple possibilities, the customer chooses an option and appreciates the outcome. The coaching skills of listening, exploring ideas, and strategizing result in calming the customer and ultimately keeping them as a customer.

For example, a coaching client was responsible for overseeing a specific project. One of the manager's on the project simply was not interested in completing their work. This coaching client was at a loss as to how to make it happen because without direct authority over the manager, it became a power struggle. In a coaching session, we explored the situation. Questions I asked included:

- How does this manager view the working relationship?
- What are the long term benefits of a good working relationship?
- How are you able to help this manager in their job or career?
- What benefit is there for this manager to complete the work?

- What approach have you taken in the past?
- What approach will you take now?

Through answering these questions, the coaching client felt they had a better understanding of what was happening and created a plan of action to move forward. Specifically, the coaching client decided on these action steps:

- Schedule time for a social lunch with the manager.
- Ask the manager what they wanted to support their work and discuss ways to help.
- At the next project meeting, ask each team member to list the benefits of completing the project successfully.
- Ask the team to list remaining action items and create a timeline.

As a result of the plan the coaching client created, they successfully rebuilt their relationship with the manager and saw results with the entire team.

As a parent imagine assigning specific chores for your son or daughter. Without coaching skills, you tell them what you want done and how to do it; most of what you say goes in one ear and out the other. With coaching skills, you recognize your son or daughter's considerations and motivations, and then ask them how chores fit within their day and have them plan how to get it done. The coaching skills of recognizing and adjusting to different personalities combined with empowering individuals to formulate their own plan of action create the buy-in of your son or daughter to follow through.

The outcome from a conflict I mediated provides perspective. Five years after their divorce a couple was still fighting and had three court cases pending. The counselor for one of them suggested mediation. The couple scheduled mediation and arrived barely speaking to one another. For two hours they talked about what they wanted and developed a plan. The couple dropped all three court cases. A year later, the counselor shared that the couple continued to communicate effectively and their plan was working. Interesting point: the plan was essentially the same plan the judge had given them five years earlier. What changed? It was their plan.

> *"What changed? It was their plan."*

Imagine helping with a community event where each of the volunteers has different ideas for how to do it and so go in a different direction. Without coaching skills, efforts are duplicated so the work is done several ways. With coaching skills, questions are asked about ideas, areas of interest, and work efforts to ensure each person is doing a different part and the camaraderie is enhanced. This results in long-term passion for the organization. The coaching skills of listening and asking questions plus adjusting to different people support teamwork and productivity.

Imagine your neighborhood association is discussing the budget and spending priorities. Without coaching skills, each neighbor voices and advocates based on personal priorities. With coaching skills, each person is asked for their ideas and thinking, pros and cons are discussed as a group, consensus is reached in most areas, and a vote is taken on a few items. Specifically, the coaching skills of exploring the options and strategizing support a neighborhood working together to achieve the best outcome for the greatest number.

A group of volunteers for a nonprofit were asked to collaborate and develop a program. To facilitate, the various sections of the program were identified and everyone was asked to volunteer in a segment. They listed individual tasks. A few volunteers then compiled the efforts of everyone into one program. One volunteer was not at the meeting and they created their own version of the program. That volunteer did not want to use the program developed by the other volunteers because they weren't involved. The volunteers that did meet were happy with the program they created together.

These examples demonstrate the value of coaching. Increasingly employees resent being told what and/or to do something, and instead prefer to know the end goal and figure out how to get there independently.
- Giving the plan takes the power away from individuals.
- Figuring out and providing a plan assumes the individual is not capable of doing it.
- Developing the plan assumes knowing better.

Coaching is based on the premise that each person is their own best expert.
- While others do have insight and experience, they have not lived the individual's life, so the insight and experience come from a different place and may not include all of the influencing factors.
- Each person has different values and priorities.
- An individual knows the people in their life and whether they will support a plan, fight it, or not care.
- Each person knows their own skills, resources, habits, opportunities, and realities at a deeper level.

Coaching supports outcomes.
- The plan's creator owns it, buys in, and follows through.
- The success or failure of a plan belongs to the creator.

How often do people use ideas suggested by others? Rarely -- typically not. When asked, people will develop their own ideas. The person who creates the plan follows through.

> *"The person who creates the plan follows through."*

COACHING PROCESS

Coaching is a process. Here is an overview of basic steps:
1. Ask an individual to list and prioritize things they want.
2. Ask them to describe their ideal.

3. Ask about obstacles to moving forward.
4. Ask them to brainstorm possible solutions from this point forward.
5. Ask about the pros and cons of each possibility.
6. Ask them which solution they want and to consider possible outcomes.
7. Ask what resources and skills they have and want.
8. Ask them to design their plan of action.
9. Support follow-through by asking what is working and what they want to adjust.
10. Celebrate progress and success.

Understanding the Power of the Coaching Process

Remember times when you have been shut down and frustrated? Remember telling someone what you wanted to no avail? Remember being asked for advice, giving great suggestions, and then learning none of your ideas were used? Coaching skills afford you the ability to listen effectively, understand others, flex to an approach that is effective, and enhance your communication process – all of which supports positive outcomes.

Consider this conversation between friends:
    Ana: Hi, how is work going?
    Bill: Okay, I guess. I wish there was an easier way to

coordinate everyone's schedule.

Ana: Why don't you just tell them the scheduled time and ask them to RSVP?

Bill: Oh no – they have to be there so we have to find a time that works.

Ana: So why don't you plan it on a set schedule?

Bill: Well, with what is happening around here there is no way that would work. Thanks anyway for the idea.

What is happening? Ana is simply unaware of the nuances of the situation so the ideas are generic in nature. With <u>coaching</u>, the premise is that the individual is their own best expert, so the approach is to listen and ask questions.

> *"...the approach is to listen and ask questions."*

Ana: Hi, how is work going?

Bill: Okay I guess. I wish there was an easier way to coordinate everyone's schedule.

Ana: How do you do it now?

Bill: I call each person and check on possible dates or availability.

Ana: What do you recommend changing?

Bill: I wish I could just talk to them all at once.

Ana: What are the options for doing that?

Bill: I don't know – this is what I am told to do.

Ana: If it works better how will everyone feel about a change?

Bill: Good, I guess.

Ana: What kinds of changes are possible?

Bill: We could schedule the next one when everyone is together in the first place.

Ana: What else?

Bill: I could email everyone simultaneously.

Ana: What else?

Bill: I could have a calendar everyone can access.

Ana: What are you going to do?

Bill: I am going to suggest to everyone when they are together that we schedule the next time then or that we have a calendar everyone can access. I think they will go for it, and if they don't I will ask if I can email everyone instead of having to call.

Ana: Seems like you really know your stuff – good idea.

Bill: Thanks.

Coaching really is this simple: instead of telling, ask.

> *"Coaching really is this simple: instead of telling, ask."*

COACHING LANGUAGE

Is coaching language a science or an art? Yes! In other words, based on research and experience, it is both. Word choice makes a difference. Consider people who are labeled as toxic or charismatic; their words are a key difference in how they are perceived.

Coaching uses clear direct language and powerful questioning, and this requires an awareness of word choices.

How clear and direct is the word *might*? The expression "coulda, woulda, shoulda all over yourself" implies limitation with each of the words. Saying *try* is giving permission not to follow through. Saying *need to* creates resistance. The words in these examples emphasize a lack of confidence and a lack of conviction or personal motivation.

Replace the limiting words *might, could, would, should, try* with **will**. Change *need* to **want** or **will**. Say the same thing with the different words and reflect on how it feels different.
- "You should apply for more jobs." Chances are the person will defend that they are applying for many jobs, and give barriers to applying for more. Alternatively, "What is your game plan for job applications?" opens the door for their proactive planning.
- "I am frustrated when I feel unheard because then it seems everything gets stuck." Using this language supports an opportunity for further discussion.
- "We should take out the garbage." Typically this is a request for a specific though unidentified person to take out the garbage because it is a one-person job. Instead,

"Please take out the garbage now," is respectful and clear.

Words make a difference and are a powerful tool for understanding, creating clear and direct communication, supporting client focus and motivation, and asking powerful questions. Equally significant is the absence of words – the power of silence.

> *"The natural tendency is to then jump in and fill that silence..."*

POWER OF SILENCE

Silence is an important tool in conversations generally and in coaching it is essential.

Think about it this way: how often have you asked a question and then been uncomfortable with the silence while waiting for an answer? The natural tendency is to then jump in and fill that silence by further explaining the question or giving possible answers. Explaining the question is unnecessary and actually indicates that perhaps the person asked is unable to figure it out for them self. Giving possible answers negates asking a question in the first place.

Alternatively, consider the other side: how often have you

wanted to say something or answer a question and been unable to either because there was no silence to talk or because before you could answer a question more was being said? Chances are you lost track of what you did want to say or simply gave up on saying anything.

Who is uncomfortable with silence, the person asking or the person thinking about the question and their answer? Silence gives the person asked an opportunity to respond, whether it is one minute or even more. (Silence becomes easier with practice.)

> *"Who is uncomfortable with silence, the person asking or the person thinking about the question and their answer?"*

LISTENING

Listening is one of the most important tasks to excel in: really hearing what is said and what is actually meant, too. When you listen well, are open and accepting, then you are prepared to engage in a coaching culture.

Interesting facts about listening:
- People hear one word in seven.
- People only remember 25 to 50 percent of what is heard.
- Only 7% of understanding is the words (55% is visual and 38% is tone / volume).

What are the techniques to move past these realities?
1. Listen intentionally and actively, completely focusing on the speaker.
2. Rephrase using the speaker's key words and put the rest in your own words to verify understanding and demonstrate you listened.
3. Reflect the emotions behind the words back to the speaker to further clarify meaning and show understanding.

How does it make a difference?   Consider this brief example:
    Eduardo: My inbox is overloaded!
    Kelly: Are you worried you cannot keep up?
This is poor listening that includes analyzing, interpreting, and judging.

Now apply effective listening:
    Kelly: Talk about your inbox.
This is opening the door to explore the situation so that the focus can be on strategizing solutions.

Friends share stories and experiences, empathize with one another, and then analyze problems and people. In conversations, friends relate to what friends say, their stories remind each other of other stories to share, plans call for input and opinion with different recommendations and advice-giving, problems call for suggested solutions.

In comparison, coaching uses listening and questioning to empower thinking, brainstorm, explore, and choose. Listening intentionally means:
- Listen to what is said with a focus on understanding thought process and interests.
- Hear the challenges and ask them to generate solutions.
- Hear the options and ask questions to empower open thinking and broader perspective.

COACHING QUESTIONS

Powerful questioning is both art and science, and involves open, probing, and clarifying questions. Because a single word potentially changes the meaning and the direction of the conversation, learning powerful questioning takes time.

For example asking, "What would you do?" falls short of creating a commitment. Instead, asking, "What will you do?" invites a client to be intentional in choosing their actions.

Consider for yourself how the same question asked two different ways makes a difference. Pause now and think about your answer to this question: What do you want? Consider where your mind goes initially, then give it more time and consider what additional thoughts occur. After a few minutes of thinking, change the phrasing of the question: What do you want in your relationships? Now the question directs you where to focus. The same occurs if instead of relationships you are asked what you want in your life or what you want in your career. The first question is truly open; the subsequent examples are questions that give direction.

The question "anything else?" invites a yes or no answer. The question, "what else?" invites consideration of additional possibilities. Close-ended questions limit thinking by either stopping additional consideration or indicating that other thoughts are best be saved for later. With open-ended questions the individual is empowered to explore, consider possibilities, and make their own choices.

> *"The question "anything else?" invites a yes or no answer. The question, "what else?" invites consideration of additional possibilities."*

Imagine a conversation where a person states, "I am overwhelmed." A follow-up question might be, "Are you worried that you are unable to handle it?" This interprets what is behind the initial statement and includes judgment. Instead ask, "What is going on?" The person then continues their thought process and shares what is happening. Overwhelmed could be overwhelmed with joy, concern, gratitude, tasks, priorities, etc. The first example of a response jumps to a conclusion, the second seeks clarification.

Imagine discussing a customer complaint. The question, "Do you think you should provide a written response?" gives an answer in the question and shuts down other options. This type of question limits thinking and possibilities. The question, "What are your possible courses of action?" empowers consideration of multiple options.

Tips for powerful question include:
- Keep it short and simple
- Ask open-ended questions
- Ask questions that focus forward
- Ask questions that are open to possibilities
- Ask questions using words that work for the individual

Powerful questioning empowers.

FOCUS AND MOTIVATION

Have you ever gotten in to an elevator and pushed the button for the floor you are already on? Without thinking, I got on at the first floor, pushed one, and waited... then pushed one again, and waited. My friend noticed and said, "Aren't we going to the fourth floor?" Amazing how much more effective it was when I pushed the right button! Often our thought process functions in the same manner: we focus on where we are, or on the problem, or on what we wish was not. It is when we choose to focus on what we do want that we see how to make it happen.

Consider this example: A work team has a big project with a tight timeline. Because of conflicts within the team, the leader decided to spend time resolving conflicts to ensure more productive efforts. The leader asked the team, "What are the problems and your needs?" The team jumped into pointing out the problems and what they needed individually, entrenching themselves in their positions. With the same group I changed the question; "how are you going to work together and get the job done?" The team realized it is their responsibility to manage differences and focused on developing solutions.

> *"How are you going to work together and get the job done?"*

People say they no longer set New Year resolutions because they will not do them anyway. At the gym, January is the busiest month of the year because many start exercising; by March it is much less crowded. Have you ever had someone tell you they will "try" and thought it was not going to happen?

In conversation, people often share what they do NOT want instead of talking about what they DO want. This focuses the attention on the past or the negative. Ask questions to create a shift so that the focus is on what is wanted. This opens the door for developing a strategy and planning. For example, when someone says they do not want to work so many hours, ask them how many hours they do want to work. Then explore options and actions for creating the change.

When people are doing something for someone else or to avoid a consequence, the impact is short term. Ask probing questions so that the individual becomes aware of their own internal motivation and what it means to them to do something. This creates long-term buy-in and motivation.

Rather than waiting for things to happen, explore with people what they do control so they develop a proactive plan moving forward. For example, when someone wants a promotion and is waiting for their review, ask what steps they can take now to move them toward earning the promotion.

Coaching creates a positive, forward focus while being proactive.

LONG-TERM IMPLICATIONS

The bottom line of what coaching means to an individual is powerful. Without coaching, how many people really take time to consider and explore their goals? How many people create effective action plans? How many people follow through with their plan? Coaching is the difference between thinking or talking about the problem versus exploring options, creating strategies, and following through.

Coaching recognizes that each person is their own best expert. Because everyone is their own best expert, coaching skills and a coaching culture creates an environment where individuals focus on possibilities and open their thinking. Coaching creates the opportunity to brainstorm and talk through different ideas, which supports effective decision making. Coaching supports people by ensuring they are intentional about their strategy and action steps. Coaching also recognizes success along the way and encourages people to acknowledge what they achieve to them self.

Imagine the impact of a culture where people focus on the future, are positive and proactive, and believe in empowering individual awareness and choice!

> *"Imagine the impact of a culture where people focus on the future, are positive and proactive, and believe in empowering individual awareness and choice!"*

Cathy Liska is the founder and CEO of the Center for Coaching Certification and the Center for Coaching Solutions.

As the Guide from the Side™, Cathy has presented, trained, and facilitated thousands of events, workshops, certification courses, and organizational retreats. She freely shares from her 20 years of experience in business ownership and management.

To ensure she continues to stay current in related fields and areas of expertise, Cathy has earned: Certified Master Coach Trainer, Certified Master Coach, Certified Consumer Credit Counselor, Real Estate Broker, Certified Apartment Manager, Certified Family Mediator, Certified Civil Mediator, Certificate of Excellence in Nonprofit Leadership and Management, Certification in the Drucker Self-Assessment Tool, Grief Support Group Facilitator, and Certified Trainer/Facilitator.

Cathy trains coaches, coaches individual clients, writes and publishes, and volunteers.

Cathy's personal mission statement is "People". She is known for her passion in sharing the insight, positive attitude, and information that supports others to achieve.

www.CenterforCoachingCertification.com

Your Office as Coaching Central
Bill Peace

Everyday Coaching Opportunities for Managers

During a typical work week, a random cross-section of any company finds various scenarios playing out: Tom is talking with one of his ambitious and responsible direct reports about advancement opportunities, down the hall Rachel is meeting with Denise about her upcoming presentation to senior management - a presentation that previously fell flat, and upstairs, Brandon asks his eager staff to brainstorm ways to streamline the broken and burdensome loan application process.

On the surface, all three vastly different workplace scenarios seem routine. What lies beneath are golden coaching opportunities with benefits for both managers and employees.

> *"What lies beneath are golden coaching opportunities with benefits for both managers and employees."*

If these three mentors and supervisors turn the routine meetings into opportunities for coaching, suddenly the sessions become much more intentional. Tom, Rachel, and Brandon can ask high impact questions, develop action plans, and follow-up with progress checks, the three main ingredients for successful coaching.

They'll use a simple process entailing the structure of a coaching conversation, coaching content, and the words or language used during these important discussions.

These three scenarios also represent a powerful way for managers to build rapport, become an accountability partner, and empower employees to flourish. Tom's employees will leave his office encouraged, Denise's confidence will be re-built, and Brandon's team will feel empowered.

Each person offers many natural and learned competencies; coaching is the single most important skill that comes to the forefront.

Let's define coaching here as a positive, intentional, collaborative discussion with the purpose of the coachee identifying and executing self-developed plans to improve, learn, achieve, and take their skill set to the next level.

Furthermore, it's a thoughtful, careful blend of process and content, as we'll soon discover.

The process, or the blueprint used to structure your conversation, consists of the wood frame of the house before the walls, sliding, or roofing. What probing questions are you asking, based your coachee's current focus? What information do you want to gather to start the building?

Then, the content of the coaching conversation fills your newly-constructed house with flooring, walls, furniture, and appliances. It's the wording, or dialogue of your interaction that gives the coachee a focal point to launch into workable actions steps.

> *"It's the wording, or dialogue of your interaction that gives the coachee a focal point to launch into workable actions steps."*

Moving past the dry disciplinary action process and redundant annual performance appraisal, today's workplace coaching addresses a wide range of topics which managers can initiate instantly in the moment, or plan over an appropriate time period.

Managers who once thought that having a sound operational track record was good enough for performing successfully and contributing to enterprise-wide goals are slowly discovering differently. They are seeking options and learning about the far-reaching benefits of coaching.

One benefit for managers includes delegation through coaching. What task, project, or action item can move off your desk to an equally, if not more, skillfully competent employee? Employees benefit because coaching hits upon one of their fundamental interests in the workplace: the opportunity to actively engage in the work they do through planning, implementing, and evaluating their outcomes. Even if they haven't come right out and directly told you this, rest assured, they're thinking it.

Coaching ranges from individual to group, from informal, creative brainstorming to more formalized, structured discussions, and from 15 minutes to a couple hours.

Managers at all levels touching every functional business area have an interest, and often the responsibility, of building strong teams in a more positive, productive work environment through coaching. In a growing number of work places, managers are measured on their coaching competency.

Recognizing everyday coaching opportunities and acting on them is crucial. As a manager who coaches, your office becomes transformed into Coaching Central, with you as the general contractor managing the entire construction or coaching process. The process includes identifying coaching opportunities, asking key questions, active listening, structuring coaching around interests and objectives, and following-up with progress checks.

> *"As a manager who coaches, your office becomes transformed into Coaching Central, with you as the general contractor managing the entire construction or coaching process."*

If there's nothing formally structured within your organization and you fully realize the positive impact of coaching, what's holding you back from initiating your own self-study or research into the effective use of coaching conversations? Today; explore and discover coaching resources that will either start you at the beginning of your journey, or help reinforce and build upon your foundation.

In this chapter, we'll take a closer look at the your everyday opportunities to coach, a simple process for coaching, plus keeping the experience positive and forward thinking. We'll hear from three coaches who use their coaching skills effectively and purposefully.

GETTING STARTED COACHING: A FRAMEWORK

So, how will you coach your staff? What if the same cross-section of the three scenarios introduced at the start of this chapter was taken at your office? What would it uncover? What coaching activities are, or could be, happening now? What do your employees want from their positions?

Tom's employee wants to advance in the company. Tom has the opportunity to become his employee's strategic partner in charting a course of action based on his employee's desires and goals for advancement.

Similarly, Rachel, Denise's manager, has the opening to have Denise positively visualize how she sees her presentation being conducted in front of senior management.

Brandon can start his meeting by asking his folks, "If we could completely redesign the lending application process, as creatively and realistically as we want, what would it look like?"

Different situations with one similar approach: What do your employees want, and what are their committed, defined, specific action steps to help them achieve those goals?

> *"What do your employees want, and what are their committed, defined, specific action steps to help them achieve those goals?"*

Turn your attention now to your staff. Think about their strengths and limitations, their specific behavior and customer or member interactions both positive and negative. Reflect on their last encounter with a customer or member, how they addressed a colleague about a sensitive topic, or when they stopped by your desk to discuss learning a new process or procedure.

What coaching opportunities exist? What opportunities are worth re-visiting? How well do you really know your staff and what motivates them? How do the opportunities you've identified match their personal and professional interests, team interests, and the bottom-line business objectives?

If you're struggling with these questions, it's all about time: yours and theirs. Minimize the Excel spreadsheet report you're working on, get up from behind your desk, and walk over to your staff. Invest the time getting to know your employees because the rewards are instrumental for long-term success.

Just as important as knowing your staff, know yourself as a coach. What are your predominant traits? How do you communicate or show up in groups?

The importance of understanding your main personality characteristics and those of your coachees is that you can now frame your coaching conversations around what resonates with the coachee. For example, when coaching someone who is outgoing and enthusiastic, perhaps their tendency is a preference for the big picture and flexibility.

Remember, it truly can be a simple process. Are you more passive or aggressive, more emotional or logical? From these four characteristics come four distinct personality styles used by the Center for Coaching Certification: Pleaser, Celebrator, Achiever, and Investigator. Other effective assessment tools include the Myers-Briggs Type Indicator® and DISC® to name just a few. If your company uses one of these tools it may be an opportunity for greater understanding.

Once you have a clearer understanding of who you are and how you operate and the same for your team members, coaching becomes an easier process. Customize your coaching style to the person sitting directly in front of you and what works best for them. Whatever approach you use to determine you and your coachee's personality style, be mindful that coaching is tailored to the individual coachee. Knowing communication styles removes the guesswork of, "Who exactly am I working with here?" and, "How do they like to be coached?"

> *"Customize your coaching style to the person sitting directly in front of you and what works best for them."*

There are both short-term and long-term gains from understanding your staff. While this type of reflection seems obvious and natural, how often does it occur?

Consider the short-term and long-term benefits of getting to know your staff or coachees. In the short-term it's fun and enlightening. It enhances your communication. It becomes easier to work together effectively. The awareness of what motivates each person is valuable. Use the results to everyone's coaching advantage. In the long-term and over time, knowing your staff well builds credibility, trust, and moves everyone forward.

In addition to having a clearer understanding of who you're coaching, take time to tap into some hidden interests of theirs many managers or mentors leave uncovered. This is a unique benefit in coaching. Mentoring differs from coaching and is a guidance and advice tool, while coaching allows the coachee to define specific goals, plot progress, and measure successes. A benefit of mentoring is learning from the personal and professional growth of another, and a benefit of coaching is personal and professional growth of the individual plus successful goal achievement.

Employees exposed to a healthy dose of both coaching and mentoring have huge advantages over their colleagues who may lack both experiences.

For example, frustrated that the organization's annual performance review wasn't giving her a more complete picture of her employee, Wendy, an information services manager, devised a list of relevant work questions to supplement her appraisal. The annual performance appraisal primarily measured work competencies and professional accomplishments over a 12-month period, then fell short of giving Wendy a more complete, employee-focused picture when it came to her coachee's desires, goals, and preferences.

The benefits of the questions, she believed, included helping her better understand the direction her employee was headed and it to serve as a roadmap for the employee's future development.

Among the short, relevant list of questions were:
- What do you like most about your job?
- If you could change one aspect of your job, what would it be and what are the reasons?
- What else do you want to accomplish in your job over the next year?

Wendy quickly realized true development success is about you knowing your employee and what makes them tick. It also demonstrates to the employee we're concerned both about how they manage their day-to-day tasks and what they want to get out of the work process, or what is in it for them.

> *"Wendy quickly realized true development success is about you knowing your employee and what makes them tick."*

"With specific questions and some of your own professional insight, you can get them where they want to go," she said, "it's really all up to them."

She also discovered how to best incent and recognize her employee, saving her from the embarrassment and frustration of doing this wrong. For example, her employee, she found, appreciated small private meetings for recognition, rather than large group, public adulation.

Coaching is also a tool that paves the way for high potential employees, those who regularly ask for coaching, who identify their wants and desires early on, and who make significant contributions over time.

THE COACHING PROCESS

Coaching is a continual process, comprised of intentional, thoughtful dialogue between a coach and coachee. While coaching sessions are all unique, even for the employees on the same work team or in the same department, the coachee is the focal point while the coach thoughtfully crafts the coaching process.

When does coaching occur? There are times when a brief, impromptu acknowledgement of progress or success is appropriate. You want to reward positive behavior for a staff member who shared a best practice on selling a new product or service with the team at last Tuesday's meeting. The result was that the brief interaction boosted the coachee's self-esteem and the team prospered from a successful example of how to confidently talk with member. Adding coaching with recognition is as simple as asking the individual how they feel about their achievement.

There are times when more thoughtful structure is appropriate for your coaching session. For example, in a coaching conversation you ask the individual coachee what they want to accomplish. Next you ask questions so they explore their possibilities, then you ask them to brainstorm their strategies, and finally you ask them their action steps. This coaching process engages and empowers the individual which in turn leads to follow-through and productivity.

Consider this example: Before going onto the playing field, does a football team simply think, "Well, let's just play our hardest and see what happens; besides we know the rules, we've won before, why bother with a plan?" Of course not! The team will practice, strategize, and plan!

Here is when coaching becomes a carefully constructed blend of process and content, as we touched upon earlier.

> *"...coaching becomes a carefully constructed blend of process and content, as we touched upon earlier."*

Process is *how* the coaching conversation plays out and how it's said; content is *what* is said, the wording and dialogue, the positive language being used.

There are many coaching formulas or action steps for coaches to use as a roadmap, perhaps the best advice is to use the one that fits you, your staff, and your organization's coaching culture.

Here's a straight-forward technique of process and content.

The process of coaching, as we've defined, is collaborative, where the listening is done by the coach, leaving most of the talking to the coachee. Common coaching process includes being supportive, establishing the desired impact of the coachee, empowering the coachee to develop action steps and plan, asking the coachee how they will move past resistance and concerns, and scheduling a follow-up to keep the coaching active.

Essentially, the content or what is said portion of coaching can be viewed as purposeful, relevant questioning. The idea is to bring the coachee to a place of inner contemplation, self-discovery, and empowerment, providing the space for them to discover their own solutions and create their own plan of action.

> *"The idea is to bring the coachee to a place of inner contemplation, self-discovery, and empowerment..."*

For example, when initiating an agreed-up plan, one which the coachee has completely designed for changes going forward, the content may sound like this:

- What are some ways your team will streamline this procedure to make it more convenient for the member?
- What are your thoughts on getting the team to work more cohesively?
- How will you approach this challenge differently in the future?

Open-ended impactful coaching questions typically start with *what* or *how*. Open-ended questions are designed to elicit responses packed with many thoughts and ideas as compared with closed-ended questions that lead and elicit short, one-word responses.

Coaching conversations culminate in the coachee setting goals for achievement. Goals take on many forms; the most commonly used format is SMART goals, an acronym for Specific, Measureable, Attainable, Relevant, and Time-Bound.

For example, a SMART goal for Brandon's team, from our opening scenario, is to brainstorm and document at least five ideas on how the department can streamline the loan application process by the 15th. The list can be reviewed and discussed to decide which ideas are feasible and can be implemented by the end of the month.

In the corporate environment, goals can be multi-level, individual, team, and enterprise-wide. Coaching plays a role in all these forms because they all typically revolve around goals and goal-setting.

So, Who's Waiting at Your Door?

High potential employees, leaders, and executives are prime candidates for in-depth coaching. They bring an eagerness, seriousness, and responsibility to their role as coachee. You may have already identified some in your organization, or they have identified themselves.

> *"High potential employees, leaders, and executives are prime candidates for in-depth coaching. They bring an eagerness, seriousness, and responsibility to their role as coachee."*

There are times when Brett, a financial institution branch manager, includes his assistant branch managers and head tellers in his managerial work. He does this to provide one-on-one and team coaching so they can experience firsthand the decision-making process and the importance of leading by example.

With his team Brett has shared how to manage performance expectations with staff, how to handle difficult conversations with members and employees, and effective goal setting with accountability built-in. He believes all these discussions fall under the vast umbrella of developing through a combination of teaching and then coaching.

"I feel that this will definitely develop them," he said. "If it's a conversation with another employee I coached them to conduct, I'll pull them aside later and ask them how it went. I always follow-up with them. What did they do well? What would they do differently?"

"This is a growth opportunity," he said. "One day this group may become managers and what better time to experience these situations than right now? This is preparing them."

Asking coachees relevant questions about where they want to be is critical. Gently and strategically guiding them to a place where they are either visualizing, listening to, feeling, or analyzing a future state of being that encompasses all of their interests is effectively coaching at a high level.

Like water in pond after a rock breaks its surface, coaching has a ripple effect. After spending time coaching an employee about a different way to handle a situation or resolving a difficult situation, you may overhear them practicing or implementing the changed behavior.

If the changed behavior has a positive effect on the coachee and he/she shares the new practice with a colleague, your initial coaching conversation has now multiplied the positive impact on its own. Your success rate as a coach has just increased and grown.

IS COACHING MEASURABLE?

Heather, one of Brett's direct reports, has this insight, "The main way I measure the outcome of a coaching session is for me to implement what was discussed during the coaching session over a period of time, and then report back to my manager and let him know how things worked for me," she says. "Also, if we discussed a specific situation and it was something that could have been handled differently, if I then experience a similar situation again, the (coaching) success measure is using the skills learned in the coaching session to handle the situation better."

> *"The main way I measure the outcome of a coaching session is for me to implement what was discussed during the coaching session over a period of time, and then report back to my manager and let him know how things worked for me."*

Knowing the coachee in the chair next to you on a deeper level is vital. It can make or break even the best planned coaching session.

President, lawyer, and architect Thomas Jefferson once said, "There is nothing more unequal than the equal treatment of unequal people." Customize your coaching session to the coachee sitting next to you.

If you apply a one-size fits all coaching style and technique to everyone, they won't understand that you think they will adapt their perspective to yours and the opportunities are limited. By the way, the coachee adapting to the style of the coach is the perfect recipe for failure. Instead, acknowledge that all coachees are different. Focus on who the coachee is as a person. Be aware of their likes and dislikes. Determine how to best communicate with them.

"You have to alter coaching, there's no cookie cutter approach," according to Susan, a lending manager. "With one of my employees, the direct route is best; laying things out in spoken bullet point is how she responds positively. On the other hand, with another employee, building self-esteem and maintaining her confidence is an essential part of the conversation," said Susan, "otherwise I've lost her completely."

> *"You have to alter coaching, there's no cookie cutter approach."*

With the employee who's empowered to make decision, and still second-guesses their choices, Susan steers them in the right direction.

"Coaching isn't criticism, it's directional guidance," she says. "It's not handing them the answers, but asking them the questions."

BE OPEN SO THAT THE COACHING CONVERSATION FLOWS

Now that you've structured your coaching session and started your discussion, the coachee may raise some unexpected concerns or topics. If it's important enough for the coachee to mention, it's important enough to bring it into the coaching session. After all, life is fluid, not stagnant.

For example, a goal mentioned a few weeks earlier may have changed due to external circumstances. Now, the coachee wants to re-visit a previously set goal to revise it. Create the opportunity for the set goal to be redefined.

When coaching for performance improvement, managers have the ability to rely on the coaching process the same as if it were a coaching session on career advancement, forming stronger inter-office relationships, or learning a new functional process.

"The challenging part (of performance improvement coaching) is the unknown," Brett says, "because sometimes you just never know where the conversation is going, or where it'll end up. Reeling employees back into the conversation and getting them to focus on the issue at hand is difficult but not impossible."

For example, some employees may be unaware that a problem exists, or you may catch them off guard when the company wants you to coach them to maintain their strengths.

The responsibility for the topic of conversation in coaching rests squarely on the shoulder of the coachee while the responsibility for effectively managing the process is that of the coach.

As long as your coaching intentions are sincere and received as genuine, your coachee will be open.

Ask:
- What are your concerns?
- You raise some legitimate issues that can be addressed outside of this meeting topic. When do you want to set-up another time for those topics?
- How does this directly affect the situation we're focusing on?

If a coachee is observed handling a situation differently based on coaching, Brett says, the coaching was successful. If they take the coaching sessions to the next level and share their new insight with others, the coaching was successful. Susan says when coachees start implementing what they share and learn that's the proof positive that coaching is successful.

Summary

Coaching opportunities are both evident and hidden. Your role as a coach is to capture the ones in front of you and go searching for the hidden treasures and golden opportunities.

Knowing your staff and appreciating their individualism is the key to unlocking the doorway to successful coaching.

The benefits of effective, workplace coaching are far-reaching, from celebrating individual accomplishments to exceeding team and corporate goals.

The coaching world is your building opportunity!

Bill Peace is the Director of Training and Development at Merck Sharp & Dohme Federal Credit Union in Chalfont, PA, where he coaches management teams on leadership development, staff enrichment programs, and sales and service training. At MSDFCU, Bill developed and continues to structure the organization's first learning and development department. Bill works with managers who want to build collaborative teams and take high potential employees to the next level.

Bill designed, implemented, and evaluated the Credit Union's first Leadership Development Program. Successful outcomes include enterprise-wide changes to expenditure deceases, revenue-generating income, and streamlined business practices during challenging financial market shifts.

For the past 15 years Bill has worked as a facilitator/seminar leader in the in the telecommunications, insurance, and personal finance industries. Bill is a Certified Professional Coach through the Center for Coaching Certification. He recently received National Credit Union Association certification in leadership and coaching for credit union sales strategies.

Bill is a national and Philadelphia Chapter member of the American Society for Training & Development, now ATD.

CLIENT-CENTERED COACHING
Tiffany Kalinka

Throughout my life I have learned and practiced many skills to better myself. The most utilized skill I have learned is to be able to relate to others and help them reach their highest potential.

Being a coach is a great way to give back and feel good about the difference you are making all at the same time. This is my passion. Cultivating a client-centered relationship is what I believe to be the key component to a productive coaching relationship. Giving yourself fully to the client is what helps them learn about themselves, set and achieve goals, and reach their greatest potential. The beauty of this is that, in turn, the success and journey your clients go through is what will give you a feeling of satisfaction as well. Everyone wins! Everyone involved accomplishes his or her goals!

> *"Being a coach is a great way to give back and feel good about the difference you are making all at the same time."*

Keeping the coaching relationship client-centered can be challenging. I have discovered and continually implement three basic strategies as an integral part in making it happen. The three ways to cultivate and keep a client-centered coaching relationship are to develop great empathy, ask open-ended questions, and become a sounding board.

PART 1: EMPATHY

As a professional coach, we have a responsibility to the client. We ensure that the client is creating their own path and making decisions based on their values and beliefs (rather than those of the coach). In order to uphold this responsibility, a coach must be able to empathize with the client. Empathy is the ability to see the situation from the client's point of view. Empathy is unlike sympathizing with someone, which means feeling compassion for them. Empathizing with the client is a great way to understand the client's perspective, gain insight into their thought process, and truly understand their core values and beliefs.

The coaching relationship is 100% client-focused. The client determines what will be discussed during sessions, defines their goals, and chooses goals on which they want to work. The responsibility of the professional coach is to keep the relationship completely client-centered and focused on what the client wants to achieve during sessions. In order to complete this task, the coach must be able to express empathy for their client.

> *"The coaching relationship is 100% client-focused. The client determines what will be discussed during sessions, defines their goals, and chooses goals on which they want to work."*

As children we are taught exercises that educate us on how to express empathy for another human being. Those same exercises can be used by the professional coach to become more empathic in their coaching practice. Empathy exercises are very beneficial to both the coach and client in the coaching relationship. Here are three exercises that help to develop our empathic abilities.

Physical Mirroring Exercises

Physical mirroring occurs naturally as part of a child's cognitive development. Children mimic the actions of adults as part of their learning. Later in life, as we more fully develop our emotions, mirroring is foundational for deeper connections with family, friends, and our social environment. It has a scientific basis in the cells found in each side of our brain known as mirror neurons. These neurons help us to see and then relate to people and the world in which we live.

The idea is to put yourself in the shoes of others by imitating their actions and experiencing their emotions. Then reflect on the experience. This exercise can be extremely beneficial to

> *"The idea is to put yourself in the shoes of others by imitating their actions and experiencing their emotions. Then reflect on the experience."*

the coaching relationship. As a coach, we want to fully understand the perspective of the client in order to be supportive and to motivate them. This exercise can be done by simple using a situation that the client has described during a session and reenacting it. For example, a client of mine described a situation where she felt afraid to ask her superior for a raise at work. After the session, I visualized the conversation she had described. Mirroring this particular situation helped me to become more aware of her perspective in regards to her relationship with her superior and what she wanted to happen.

> *"As a coach, we want to fully understand the perspective of the client in order to be supportive and to motivate them."*

EMOTIONAL MIRRORING EXERCISE

Emotional mirroring is copying the emotions of another person in order to better understand what emotions the person is feeling in regards to what they are communicating. The emotional mirroring exercise is especially useful with clients who are experiencing deep emotions. Ask questions about their circumstances now to identify barriers and be aware of the emotions. Afterwards imagine you are them during that conversation and imitate them as accurately as possible. Then assess how you feel about the emotions you just experienced. From that assessment, consider different possibilities about their emotions and how they are being influenced. Ideally you can ask them later if you are accurate.

ACTIVE LISTENING

Active listening is intentionally listening with all of the senses, focused on really hearing and understanding everything that the client is attempting to express. At a deeper level is reflective listening where you feed back what emotions you are perceiving to verify understanding. This helps both the client (for clarity and validation) and the coach (for more complete understanding).

> *"Active listening is intentionally listening with all of the senses, focused on really hearing and understanding everything that the client is attempting to express."*

It can be tempting to want to speak up during a coaching session; at the same time, the responsibility of the coach is to truly listen to what is being said by the client. This exercise is extremely beneficial. In this exercise listen intentionally; practice until it becomes natural.

Active Listening Exercise: Listen intentionally, with all of your senses, to another person. Focus on what they say specifically, their intended meaning, and their feelings behind the words. Rephrase or summarize their words back to them and reflect the perceived emotions. (This provides them clarity in their thinking plus lets them know you are listening and understanding.) Ask clarifying questions for full understanding. Lean forward and nod to let the speaker know you're listening.

Forget your view of the situation and listen only to what the client is saying instead of thinking about your personal insights. If you are waiting to say something then you are not listening.

These simple exercises are known to teach children to learn to empathize, and are also extremely helpful in expanding the minds of adults. They help us to establish trusting and healthy relationships with our clients. The relationship between the coach and the client is stronger and more productive when empathy is expressed by the coach.

> *"The relationship between the coach and the client is stronger and more productive when empathy is expressed by the coach."*

PART 2: OPEN-ENDED QUESTIONING TECHNIQUES

The skill of asking truly open questions is valuable in many career fields such as teaching, sales, mental health, and conflict mediation. Powerful questioning is a core competency for professional coaching. An open-ended question invites fuller reflection and expression. The opposite is a closed question, which can be answered with a word or two. An example of a closed ended question is, "Are you happy with your current job?" This question limits the client, because it only gives the client two options. They can either answer yes or no. As coaches we want to give the client opportunities to express their thoughts. Instead of using the closed ended question above, a coach might ask, "How do you feel about your current job?" or "What do you think of your current job?" These questions open the door for the client to give many answers, be descriptive, and also to explore the possible goals they want to accomplish at work. Open-ended questions are freeing and empowering.

As professional coaches, we want all of our questions to be open-ended. We want to be able to receive as much information from our clients as possible in order to fully understand them and assist them as their coach. Many of us have grown accustomed to asking closed-ended questions or limiting questions that pull little useful information from the conversation. These are habits that can be challenging to change and it is possible. There are tools and techniques that are very useful to coaches in order to ask the question that will be most beneficial to the client.

LIMITING VERSUS POWERFUL WORDS OR PHRASES

There are many words that we use in our daily language that are limiting and often we go through our day using them without realizing the effect they are having on us or others. These words limit our thoughts, our ability to be creative, and our sense of possibility. Words or phrases such as can't, couldn't, need, would, or not are limiting. For example: I can't afford it, I don't have a choice, I don't have any say, I need to, and I would. Instead, powerful words or phrases help us to stay positive, goal-driven, and determined. For example: I will, I can, I am, I have the skills, and I want. Erasing limiting phrases from our vocabulary can be frustrating as we are hardly aware that we are using them. Changing a habit takes time and consistent practice. We can change our language to a more powerful one if we become aware of our word choice and use techniques to practice substituting limiting words for positive, more powerful words and phrases. If we use the techniques consistently and repetitively, we can change the habit and have a more positive perspective.

There are techniques that can help us practice replacing limiting language with positive and powerful language. This will both help us better ourselves and as coaches help us ask more powerful open-ended questions.

VISUAL REMINDER

Visualization is extremely beneficial when we want to change a habit. Specifically, when we want to replace limiting words with positive ones, visualization techniques can help to move the process along. First, make a list of all the positive words and phrases that you know or find. Make many copies of the list and place the list in places that you visit daily. For example, in your home, office, and any other location you look at often throughout the day. Be aware of what you think and say throughout the day and look at your list. If you hear yourself using limiting language replace it with words from your list. Review your list daily and use it as motivation to stay positive. (Notice that writing down the limiting language is not a part of the exercise. Completely erasing limiting language from your thought process requires that you don't see it at all in your daily activities.)

"Be aware of what you think and say throughout the day..."

MEDITATION

Meditation is a very powerful tool, one that has been around for many years and is used across all walks of life. The ultimate purpose of meditation is to find balance by becoming mindful. So many thoughts can occur in one's mind throughout a single day, leaving one to feel stressed, overwhelmed, and tired. Through meditation, you have a chance to quiet the mind and focus on breathing. This takes a lot of practice. Once mastered, you will see things more clearly and be able to focus on others, which is amazingly helpful in the coaching relationship.

There are many great uses for meditation including the incorporation of positive language into our thought process. A simple focused breathing for 10 to 15 minutes as a meditation helps you to relax, find balance, and think positive. Meditation takes time and practice in order to find balance.

One technique that I use when meditating is to visualize my thoughts floating down a river. When a negative thought arises in my mind, I acknowledge it, and then visualize that thought floating away. This technique helps me to acknowledge my thoughts while staying focused on the positive.

Meditation helps us to understand our own thinking and our feelings. It guides us and is a tool for transforming our focus toward the positive, peaceful, and happy. This is a powerful tool that can be used throughout your day to become aware, both of changing how you think and how you speak as well. In turn, the way in which you ask questions will become more powerful.

PART 3: BECOMING A SOUNDING BOARD

In the coaching business we want to be sounding boards for our clients. What exactly is a sounding board? A sounding board is a person whose reactions to someone else's ideas are used as a test of their likely success before they are put into action. As coaches, we want our clients to feel free to express their thoughts and ideas. We want them to feel that they are in a safe environment and they can trust us with the information they choose to reveal. In order to be a true sounding board we must refrain from expressing our opinions. This can be difficult as we naturally have opinions and feel the desire to express them. In the coaching relationship, the most efficient and productive sessions are accomplished when we eliminate our opinions from the conversation and become true sounding boards for our clients. Several tools help.

GUIDED MEDITATION

Guided meditation is a tool that utilizes the goals of the client in a written format. The client listens to the written meditation repetitively, which allows them to fully believe in their goals and work towards achieving them. In my experience as a coach, the use of a guided meditation has been extremely beneficial in regards to becoming a sounding board for my clients. The guided meditation utilizes reflective listening, rephrasing, and meditation. The entire wording of the meditation is derived from the words of the client. My clients have told me that after hearing the guided meditation read to them, they were surprised to hear the actual words they used in sessions throughout the meditation. They stated that this made them feel like they were really being heard and that I understood what they were wanting to say and what they wanted to accomplish. I have also been coached and had a guided meditation written for me. After listening to it, I was able to gain perspective on my goals and what I really wanted to accomplish through my coaching sessions. The guided meditation was a true reflection of my thoughts and hearing them out loud gave me the support to continue to move forward. The guided meditation is a great tool to help build a strong relationship between the coach and the client. It also assists you as a coach in becoming a great sounding board.

REPHRASING

Rephrasing is a tool we use often as coaches. Its primary purpose is to let the client know that we are truly listening. It is also useful when to become sounding boards for our clients. When we feel the urge to express our opinions, we instead can reflect on what the client is actually saying. Using the clients own words, we then rephrase what was said and say it back to them. In this way we show them we are truly aware and attentive to them, we are bouncing their ideas back to them, and we are validating their thoughts and ideas. It is important to utilize the descriptive words that the client states. For example, a client might describe their current relationship by saying, "I really enjoy spending time with him." If you rephrase this statement for the client by changing the word "enjoy" to "love" it changes the statement entirely. This might seem like a simple replacement of words; it could be significant to the client. It could completely change the meaning of the statement for the client. Rephrasing using the descriptive words of the client is extremely beneficial. It is a powerful tool in the coaching profession.

ACTIVE LISTENING

As coaches we utilize our active listening skills throughout the coaching sessions. We use active listen to confirm what we have heard and moreover, to confirm the thoughts of the client. Active listening helps us to replace our opinions with reflection, paraphrasing, and rephrasing. We focus solely on the client and what the client wants the sessions to be about. Following are tools that help us better our active listening skills in order to better serve our clients.

PAY ATTENTION

Give the client your full attention and actively acknowledge their ideas. Remember, non-verbal communication also carries meaning. Put aside distracting thoughts. Thinking ahead and preparing for coaching sessions is extremely beneficial. Have the tools you utilize ready to go. Make sure your other phone lines, or personal cell phone ringer, are turned off. These noises can both distract the client and can make them feel that they do not have your undivided attention. Avoid being distracted by environmental factors and listen to the inflection in the client's voice. This is crucial and can tell you a lot about the client's interests and wants.

PROVIDE FEEDBACK

What we hear can be distorted by our personal beliefs and assumptions. As a listener and as a coach, it is your responsibility to fully understand. Actively listen, rephrase, reflect, and ask clarifying questions. Reflect what has been said by paraphrasing. "Sounds like you are saying," is a great reflective phrase. Ask questions to clarify such as "What does that mean to you?" Occasionally summarize the client's conversation as well.

I recently worked with a client who was having difficulty balancing her job, raising her children, and going to school. She had many goals that she wanted to achieve and talked very fast. I found it beneficial to clarify with her often in order to stay on the same page. I summarized what she was saying and ask questions such as, "What does balance mean to you?" or "What does structure mean to you?" These questions helped me to understand her perspective. This showed I was listening and that I was understanding her thought process.

STAY FOCUSED

Although interrupting may seem to be inappropriate, it is appropriately used in coaching to maintain focus. Be intentional about interrupting by knowing when it is useful and when to listen while the client finishes expressing their thoughts.

There are times when interruption is helpful to the coaching session. I have had two clients that I found interrupting beneficial to the relationship. I interrupted with open ended questions in order to clarify and stay focused. Neither client found it to be offensive. It actually helped the clients to stop and reflect on what they were saying, and to take a moment to organize their thoughts. It allowed me as the coach to follow their thought process, stay focused, and continue to understand their perspectives.

> *"Although interrupting may seem to be inappropriate, it is appropriately used in coaching to maintain focus."*

Allow your mind to create a mental model of the information being processed throughout the session. Be aware and stay in the moment by using mental pictures. They can be literal or abstract as long as they keep you focused on the client and what they are expressing. Concentrate on and remember key words and phrases.

Relax

The coaching process requires a certain amount of multi-tasking. While listening, taking notes, and asking the right questions, you can become overwhelmed. Everything that we do as a coach takes practice. Once these techniques become natural the process begins to flow and you are able to simply be present and attentive. The natural flow of the coaching session takes time and practice. I coach and am coached as often as possible. If I have a period of time where I have few coaching clients, I ask friends if I can coach them for the experience. I also have a coach. The experience of being coached has helped me to better my abilities and to accomplish the goals I set in my own life. This has also helped me to relax in my sessions as a coach. The more I practice and work with my own coach, the more natural coaching becomes to me. My ability to be a sounding board becomes more innate as I gain experience coaching. Your ability to be a sounding board to your client will enhance the sessions and build the relationship between you and your client.

> *"The experience of being coached has helped me to better my abilities and to accomplish the goals I set in my own life."*

Conclusion

The tools described above are the most efficient ways to cultivate the client-centered coaching relationship. Empathy, open-ended questioning, and being a sounding board make the coaching relationship stronger, more productive, and more beneficial to both the client and the coach.

Becoming well-versed and practicing these strategies in daily life will, in turn, help you acquire the skills to coach. Ultimately, the prescribed tools are beneficial for all aspects of life as well as the coaching relationship. Utilizing them as often as possible will help them become a normal part of your mind-set, thus strengthening your coaching ability too.

Becoming a coach has been a dream of mine for many years. I have long had the desire to work with people on achieving their goals. As I continue to coach and be coached, I love the experience even more. Coaching has both given me a chance to support people in achieving their goals and it has supported me in becoming more open-minded, more positive, and more productive. I have learned many things from the coaching experience with the most important being the focus on the client. The impact that coaching has had on me as both the coach and the client has been significant and extremely worthwhile.

Tiffany Kalinka is the founder of Silver Lining Coaching Services, LLC. Through many of life's trials and tribulations, she has learned to embrace change and commit to her continual growth. Her ultimate goal is to motivate and support others in doing the same.

Tiffany is known for being positive, open-minded, understanding, and creative. She is extremely goal-driven and her perseverance is evident. The time and effort she has put forth in expanding her life skills and knowledge is admirable. In addition to her certification as a professional coach, she has obtained certification in computer technology. She holds a master's degree in clinical psychology with an emphasis on assessment and goal-setting. With a minor in cultural anthropology, Tiffany has long been interested in other people, different cultures, and lifestyles. One of her philosophies in life is to live and let live. Her efforts are client-centered as she is eager to support and embrace each individual.

Tiffany is married with one son. She enjoys reading, writing, traveling, and most of all learning. Learning about others and helping her clients reach their goals is, in turn, what motivates Tiffany. Her personal mission statement is exactly the words she lives by each day, "It is not over when you fail, it is over when you quit."

CREATING YOUR PERSONAL STRATEGIC PLAN
Pamela Howard

In my former professional life, I worked as an administrator at many different non-profit organizations. During my tenure, one of the chores that we often worked on was a long-term strategic plan. The board of directors, executive staff, and usually an outside consultant worked for months on a long and cumbersome document. Many times, the document was completed, filed away, and not looked at again; the next time we looked at it was when it was time to write a new one.

Alternatively, good things can happen when the process of writing a great plan meets the intended end results. A well written strategic plan is a living document that serves as a guide for moving an organization, a business, or, in this case, a person forward, especially during times of change or expansion. Professionally, just like in our personal lives, things can happen that call for changes to even the best written plan.

> *"A well written strategic plan is a living document..."*

I know this first hand. In my personal life, I lost my husband at age 51 to a massive and sudden stroke. Four months after that, my ex-husband took his own life. Four months after that my Mother passed away suddenly. My husband was my best friend and he was also my business partner. Every aspect of my life was thrown into turmoil with many huge, life-altering decisions to make. I found myself feeling utterly lost and untethered from everything that had anchored my life. The plan that my husband and I had created for our lives and our business was now null and void. I was devastated, sad, alone, and reluctantly considered creating a new plan.

The plan that I developed with my life coach over the next several months was the course of action that got me to where I am today. My plan is a living document with realistic goals, timelines, wants, objectives, and strategies that has helped me to move forward through the most difficult time of my life. Even today, when faced with a new opportunity, I review my plan and use the tools to help me move forward with my decision making.

I was very fortunate that I had a client and friend who was an outstanding and well respected executive coach. She was the person you went to when you wanted to make a major career change or get that next big promotion. She made an exception and offered to become my coach. She wanted to help me find a new path to my new life. She was personally, as well as professionally, vested in my success. The methods she employed as a coach empowered me to define my starting point, and to create the vision for the new life I wanted. She guided me to put it all down on paper for execution. This was exactly the right thing for me at the time. I was a new life coach myself and it was the best on-the-job training and example of coaching that I could have ever experienced. I want to pay if forward by helping others in the same way.

I will lead you through the steps of determining your starting point to create a personal strategic plan. It is an examination of where you are right now and defining your destination. Your destination will be determined by your answers to the following questions:
- Where do I want to be?
- What do I want my new life to look like?

You will create a vision with images to help guide you on your way. You will write a personal mission statement to define how you want to live your life. Finally, you will set the goals and objectives to build your road map to success.

Before you start the process of creating your personal strategic plan, gather the following supplies. All are inexpensive and easily purchased at almost any department store:
- A good pen for writing. Keep this pen with the journal you will also be acquiring. Keep them handy for writing at any time of the day or night.
- A journal or notebook. Purchase something in your favorite color, or a nice pattern that is appealing. Select something that you will enjoy writing in each day. Select a size that is transportable.
- A large poster board to create your Vision Board.

- A glue stick to affix items to your Vision Board.
- Old magazines to cut motivational pictures, sayings, and articles from to make your Vision Board.

"Begin by determining your current personal starting point."

STEP 1: DEFINE YOUR STARTING POINT (WHERE ARE YOU NOW?)

Where do you start the process of creating a personal strategic plan? Begin by determining your current personal starting point. The first step is a writing assignment to determine where your life is right now. Please answer the following questions in your new journal:

1. Where is my life right now?
2. What do I like and what do I want to change?
3. What are the most important or critical changes that I want to make in my life?
4. What are the obstacles that keep me from living / achieving the life I want?
5. What are my support systems that are in place to help me make changes in my life?

The answers to these questions will begin to lay the groundwork for change. Take your time in answering these questions. In this process, I have found that the more time you spend writing your thoughts, the easier it will become to write your feelings and ideas. The process will start to become more natural and top of mind, and new and different ideas will come more freely. It's perfectly normal to have many conflicting ideas when you start the process. Keep writing them all down and the ideas and answers will be sorted and prioritized later.

Also remember that your journal is just that, yours. Your answers are yours alone. There are no wrong answers and you do not have to ever show your writings to anyone. What you write is strictly confidential and is completely your own unless you choose to share it.

"...define the vision of where you want to be."

STEP 2: DEFINE YOUR DESTINATION (WHERE DO YOU WANT TO BE?)

You cannot make changes in your current life if you don't know what that new life looks like. In this next phase, we will take the answers to your previous questions and begin to build on them to define the vision of where you want to be.

Please answer these questions in your journal:
1. If I could have any life I wanted, what would it be? (Be limitless and go a little crazy here!)
2. In more realistic terms, what is the life I really want?
3. What change(s) I will make to get to the destination?

4. Where do I see myself one year from now?
5. How will this new situation really make me feel?

Include in your answers how this new life or change will look, feel, taste, and smell. What does the new house look like? What will your health be like? Where will your new office be? What will the new career feel like and how much money will you be making? Write down as many specifics as are appropriate to your destination.

When you are answering these questions, be sure to take as much time and space as you want. The idea is to expand thinking by giving yourself freedom with time and space. Imagine every detail of your new life or situation.

Once you have answered these questions and you have the beginnings of a vision for the new you, have a little fun and make the vision more real by creating a vision board. The vision board will be a real representation of your new life. As they say, "a picture is worth a thousand words," and the vision board is a tangible symbol of where you are headed. A vision board, in its most simple terms, is a collage created to represent the things you want to have, the things you want to be, or the things you want to achieve in your life.

To begin, look through magazines and on-line resources such as Pinterest to search for pictures, motivational quotes, and other visuals that represent what you want your life to be. Is there a picture of a corner office? Is there a picture of your next house? Can you find a picture of a marathoner finishing a race? Is there a picture of that beach you have always wanted to visit? Find quotes and sayings that express your emotions and the emotions you want to have. Find pictures of the life and experiences that you want to attract. Clip out whatever is most meaningful to you and represents where you want to be. Choose pictures and words that are uplifting, inspiring, and affirming. Please know that you can use markers or paint to write those words or sayings on your board as well. However you want to create it, do it!

As you collect these pictures and quotes, etc., start gluing them to the poster board in whatever manner is visually pleasing to you. Again, this is like the journal – there are no wrong answers! This vision board is for you and you alone. It only has to please you. I do suggest that if you are working on more than one area of your life, consider dividing the board into sections: one for personal, one for professional, one for family, or whatever works for you.

While you are working on your vision board, and especially after it is complete, put it in your home or office in a place where you can see it each and every day. By looking at your board, you are reinforcing in your mind what you want your life to look like on a daily basis. Sit with your board, study it, and feel free to change it as your thoughts and dreams change throughout this process. As with your overall plan, your vision lives and changes.

> *"...your vision lives and changes."*

STEP 3: BUILD YOUR ROAD MAP (HOW WILL YOU GET THERE?)

Now that you have had a chance to do some personal introspection through answering questions and creating your vision board, it's time to create the roadmap that will get you to the changes you want. The next step is to write your personal mission statement that will assist you in setting goals and objectives to complete your personal strategic plan.

What is a personal mission statement? A mission statement is a few concise sentences that define your sense of purpose and define how you live your life. Your mission statement can guide you and let others know what your innermost values are as a person. My personal mission statement is, "To live my life to the fullest of my ability, both personally and professionally." While these mission statements are quite short and to the point, they capture the essence of the authors. This is what a good personal mission statement is about. It brings your life into extreme focus for yourself and for those around you.

To begin to write your personal mission statement, look back to the questions you answered in Step 1 and Step 2. Reread where you are and where you want to be. The answers you wrote about where you want to be will give you clues to how you want to live your new authentic life.

To begin to write your mission statement follow these steps and use your journal to make notes.

- Define your personal core values. In other words, what are the most important traits that make you tick and make you who you are? Make an inventory of the qualities you like the best about yourself and the ones you want to focus on.

This is the time to be completely honest with yourself. The values that you are writing about can also be values that you want to develop more as part of your new plan. This is the time to clarify your priorities. Be sure to write down both personal and professional qualities and values that make you who you are

- Begin to draft sentences using the traits, values, and qualities that you want to be known for and will help to move you forward. Continue to write drafts until you have a mission statement that you are happy with.

Like any of the parts of this project, the mission statement is not carved in stone by any means. It is a moving target that can and will change as you move forward with your life.

The last step with your mission statement is to write it in several places that you will see every day. Perhaps put it in your calendar or planner, on a sticky note on the bathroom mirror (this is a good place because it may be the first and last thing you see each day), put a copy on the dashboard of your car, put a copy on an index card in your office; wherever it will be the most effective reminder for you.

Now that you have answered questions, completed your vision board, and written your mission statement, you will have a pretty good idea of where you currently are and where you want to go. Your destination will be clearer. You will be aware of what is important to you and the changes you will to make to get there. Now it is time to develop the meat of your plan, the goals and objectives to get to your destination.

Goals are what you want to achieve generally. They will be integrated with your mission and vision. A goal ideally meets the following criteria:
- Suitable: Does it fit with your mission and vision?
- Acceptable: Does it fit with your values and those of the people around you that it affects, i.e. your family, loved ones, co-workers?
- Understandable: Is it clear and easy to understand?
- Flexible: Is it adjustable based on other changes?

Below are examples of personal or professional goals:
- Improve my overall health
- Spend more time with my family

- Get a better job
- Be financially secure
- Write that book I have always wanted to

Ensure your goals focus on the aspects of your life you want to change. It is recommended to begin with a manageable number of goals. It is easy to become overwhelmed with too much change too quickly. Once you have reached success with a goal(s), you can set additional ones.

Objectives are specific and quantified statements of what you want to achieve and when you want to achieve. Objectives are achievement milestones along the road. Your objectives will be:
- *Measurable*: What will I do and by when?
- *Suitable*: Does it match up to my vision and goals?
- *Feasible*: Is it possible?
- *Commitments*: Am I committed?

Examples of objectives:
- To reach my weight goal in the next 6 months.
- To put $5,000 into savings over the next year.
- To have a new job within the next three months.
- To write 5 chapters of my book over the next 6 months.

Now that you have written your goals and objectives, consider the strategies that you will use to reach these goals. Strategies are the approach for how you will achieve a goal. A strategy includes actions or activities in series designed by you to achieve your goal. Define milestones for measuring success of your goals and objectives within your strategy for achieving your vision. A strategy is the stepping stone to each goal.

> *"Define milestones for measuring success..."*

Examples of strategies are:
- Join a gym to exercise at least three times per week.
- Take my coffee/lunch to work every day and put the money I normally spend into my savings account.
- Meet with a career coach to assist in finding a new job.
- Make an appointment to meet with a writing coach for support to start my book.

The more specific you are with your strategies the better. Write down exactly when you are starting your new strategy, how often you are doing it, and for how long. When you are specific you are committing to your goal.

> *"When you are specific you are committing to your goal."*

STEP 4: TRACKING YOUR PROGRESS AND EVALUATION

Questions to ask:
- Am I making progress toward my goals and objectives being achieved? If yes, reward yourself. When you

complete a goal is a good time to set the next goal(s) because you have more to accomplish.

- If goals and objects have not been met according to the timeframe you have set for yourself, ask yourself the following:
    - What deadlines for completion will I change?
    - How do I ensure balance with the number of goals I set for myself?
    - What are the resources (money, equipment, facilities, training, etc.) to achieve the goals?
    - How do I ensure my goals and objectives are realistic?
    - What priorities will I change to put more focus on achieving the goals?

If your goals have not been achieved in the timeframe you originally set forth, this is an opportunity for reflection. This is a learning experience about how change affects you. Be kind to yourself. Turn to your journal to determine what can be learned from the experience in order to move toward the end results you are looking to achieve. Begin again. There is value in starting from the beginning and reworking your plan.

As part of your self-evaluation process, your journal is an excellent way to document your progress and achievements. Journaling may be a short paragraph logging what you did and what happened. You can also use your journal to list what you ate and what exercise you did, how you're feeling, and any specific events or influencing factors. Do this daily and be specific for the best results.

What I enjoy most about my journaling experiences is looking back to see how far I have come from where I started. Looking back at my cryptic lists and early goals that I had written, and seeing them turn into real goals, objectives, and strategies that I was actually able to make happen is incredibly gratifying. The act of journaling my feelings and experiences was also a wonderful personal and private outlet for the challenges that can come along with making great change.

> *"What I enjoy most about my journaling experiences is looking back to see how far I have come from where I started."*

THE PROCESS OF CHANGE

The process of creating what is described above can help you create your personal road map to success. To be successful in changing your life, it is imperative to know where you currently are, where you want to go, and most importantly, how to get there. Think of your new journal that is full of answered questions, goals, objectives, and strategies as a living, breathing toolbox that you have created just for you. It is a blue print to your new life, and it is a wonderful gift to give to yourself. Change is challenging and can be hard and scary. There are different kinds of change. There is the change that we want to achieve, like a new job, or a weight goal. Then there is the change that happens to us, for example in my case, a death made it necessary for me to change almost every part of my life, both personally and professionally. The steps that I have taken you through above will work for both kinds of change.

As you start working your plan, be sure to reward yourself for achieving even the smallest of milestones. Did you join the gym? Give yourself a gift of relaxation time. Did you go to the gym regularly for two weeks? Buy yourself a new workout outfit. Did you make an appointment with the career counselor? Buy a new shirt or blouse to wear to the interview you know you will get. Instead of beating yourself up over a lapse, ask: How do you want to adapt the steps in your new strategy? How will you maintain a positive, can-do attitude? Your thinking creates your results, so instead of being disappointed when something doesn't happen, ask yourself questions about how to refocus and flex. Be open to the possibilities: change your goals, rethink your goals, and/or rethink your strategies.

Think about what's at stake if you stay the same and refocus on your lists. Think about how it will feel, the benefits, and the value of incorporating your chosen changes into your life. Make the commitment to begin now and follow through.

Pamela Howard founded At Your Service in March 2006 with her late husband Michael Howard. What started as the only successful personal concierge service in Albany became AYS Coaching and Consulting. The business model, priorities, and focus shifted as Pamela's personal life changed after the sudden passing of her husband.

Pam has over 20 years of experience with not-for-profit organizations including the New York State museum, Hope House, Albany Institute of History and Art, Albany Boys & Girls Club and Regional Food Bank. Pam has been nationally recognized for bringing Senator Hillary Clinton to the Albany Boys & Girls Club and for spearheading the pilot program of the national "One Campaign" fundraising program.

Pam is a graduate of the Albany Colonie Chamber's Capital Leadership program, Entrepreneur Assistance program, and has been a GenNext mentor. She is Chairman of the Leukemia and Lymphoma Society annual "Taste of Compassion" wine event, and serves on their board. Pamela was the first recipient of the Leukemia and Lymphoma Society's "Michael Howard Spirit Award" in 2013.

PHoward@AYSAlbany.com

COACHING FOR LEADERSHIP
Patti Oskvarek

How can a coach help clients become excellent leaders? In this chapter I will discuss a variety of techniques, tools, and methods coaches can use to support their clients. In doing so I will offer solid examples of these processes in action the client can draw on and emulate to develop greater leadership abilities in their own work environments. Now let's get started on the journey to discover how to coach client's to become excellent leaders.

COACHING CLIENTS TO BUILD GOOD RAPPORT

Every coaching relationship must establish a good rapport in order to create an environment that supports growth and success. Building trust is also an important part of developing a good rapport in any relationship and is essential in coaching. This is particularly true when coaching clients to become excellent leaders. An effective coach models this with their client/leaders, which encourages the client to do the same with those with whom they interface. Understanding how to establish good rapport is a key step to becoming a superior leader, and this begins with developing good listening skills.

> *"Understanding how to establish good rapport is a key step to becoming a superior leader, and this begins with developing good listening skills."*

COACHING CLIENTS TO PRACTICE AND PARTICIPATE IN ACTIVE LISTENING

If your client actively engages with co-workers or leads others in any capacity, an element of coaching will benefit their interactions. You may explore a variety of active listening techniques as a way of helping your clients improve their leadership abilities. As a coach, active listening will help build a healthy relationship with your client. For the client, becoming more deeply aware of and working on the skill of active listening will enhance communication with others in the workplace and in their personal lives. Consider sharing various resources with your clients and support them to practice active listening techniques with their staff members. These easy but powerful techniques can prove useful in building stronger relationship between your clients and their staff. Active listening encourages and allows others to speak and convey their wants, objectives, and concerns. The ability to proficiently listen and build positive work relationships with co-workers and others demonstrates engagement and is the core of strong leadership skills.

Active Listening Techniques for You and Your Client
- Be silent when the client is speaking.
- Keep an open mind.
- Watch your body language.
- Watch her body language.

- Listen for key words and full understanding of their meaning.
- Be prepared to ask short, direct questions to gather deeper understanding of key words.
- Paraphrase what was said and ask if it is understood.
- After the client has expressed what she wants to tell you, ask other questions to ensure you truly understand what she stated.
- Ask open-ended questions to empower the client to come up with solutions and a plan of action.

The intention is build trust by listening deeply so the client opens up and discusses her challenges. She will come up with her own solution. Asking the right questions and probing deeper will help move the client towards finding the outcome that is right for her. Be aware that you do not provide the client with what you think the outcome should be. When the client discovers, on her own, how to proceed with a solution, she is more apt to implement it.

- Discuss what steps the client will take and the timeline to achieve each step to accomplish the solution.
- Each time you meet with your client ask what she has accomplished towards her goals.

"The intention is build trust by listening deeply so the client opens up and discusses her challenges."

It has been my experience that clients are excited to talk about their progress and what they have accomplished. They feel proud and are happy to be able to report that they are making headway towards their goals.

COACHING CLIENTS WHO ARE HAVING DIFFICULTY MOVING FORWARD

If a client is having difficulty moving forward, start by asking questions about the situation. Help him dissect the situation to learn the reasons he feels immobilized. What is the obstacle in his way? When a client believes he has found a possible solution, he will be encouraged to set his focus towards the goal.

> *"When a client believes he has found a possible solution, he will be encouraged to set his focus towards the goal."*

Questions to ask when your client is immobilized:
1. What is holding you back?
2. Where does the hesitation come from?
3. How will you move past these obstacles?
4. What resources do you have?
5. What resources do you want?
6. What actions will you take?
7. When will you take them?
8. How will you make them happen?
9. What are your action steps now?

COACHING LEADERS ON TIME MANAGEMENT

Time management is important to all of us in this busy world. It is an essential tool for leaders in the workplace. A good coach will help clients explore how time management is working, or not working, for them by evaluating the following items:
- Identify long and short-term goals.
- Create a daily, weekly, and monthly to do list.
- Recognize what can be achieved.
- Plan enough time for urgent matters and interruptions.
- Schedule uninterrupted time for important tasks.
- Minimize stress by avoiding over-committing.

Effective time management is an essential skill for client/leaders to master for their future success.

COACHING LEADERS TO JOURNAL

Journaling is a good technique for clients to use when working through challenging situations. When a client becomes frustrated or emotional, a coach may explore writing as a way of working through the experience. Journaling is a powerful way to release the negative thoughts and feelings we tend to bottle up inside. Coach your client to find their ideal place, a quiet spot or in his office with the door closed. He can write down all his feelings and what elements are challenging him about the situation. Once those angry and negative thoughts are out of his head and onto a piece of paper or in a journal where he can revaluate and reflect upon them, the client may be able to more easily move forward, and refrain from making the situation worse by being reactive. This technique is a stress management tool and empowers the client to move pro-actively towards a positive solution to his problem. The client may choose to keep this writing private in a locked, safe place or destroy it if there is any concern about breach of privacy.

Journaling may be used to work out specific problems, generate ideas, and for brainstorming. Writing down thoughts, ideas, and feelings can help release tension and encourage creative thinking. This kind of writing can help clients come up with solutions, new ideas for products, and improve customer service techniques. Focusing on the idea or product through journaling can challenge the client to discover creative solutions. Ask your client powerful questions to help him open up and find new ways of approaching the situation. Then, offer him time on his own to reflect on possible solutions.

Questions to Consider When Journaling to Release Tension and Achieve Clarity:
1. What happens if you react right now, at this moment?
2. What will happen if you decide not to react?
3. What are the benefits of walking away and taking time to reflect before handling the situation?

4. How can you handle this situation in a calm manner?
5. How will you overcome obstacles in the way?
6. After you have time to reflect, how will you respond?
7. What are your action steps now?

Journaling and spending time in self-reflection helps to build a client's confidence and can assist him to discover a plan of action. With a self-implemented action plan, he is more likely to succeed and achieve what he really wants. Also, the client will be better prepared to handle questions and concerns about the situation, which can facilitate a much smoother transition to a positive resolution.

> *"Journaling and spending time in self-reflection helps to build a client's confidence and can assist him to discover a plan of action."*

COACHING LEADERS ON BUILDING TRUST RELATIONSHIPS

As mentioned earlier, a client who knows how to build trust relationships with members of her staff is on her way to building a strong foundation as a leader. As her coach, you can initiate this process by asking questions about the kind of interaction she now has with her staff. Having already established the importance of practicing good listening skills, you can give her the opportunity to evaluate, for herself, how she is doing. By listening well and consistently she can draw others to her, and foster loyalty and trust in her relationships. Model this, using

your coaching skills, giving her your complete attention and focusing on what she shares. Then ask the client several questions to clarify her evaluation. Examples include:
- What type of relationship do you want with your staff?
- How do you want to improve your relationship?
- What does building trust with your staff mean to you?
- What does building trust mean to them?
- What characteristics do you admire in other leaders?
- Which of these characteristics do you want to develop?
- How will you incorporate these characteristics?
- What are your actions steps?
- What are the benefits to making this work?

These kinds of questions will open the client's thinking process towards creating change and the opportunity to build respect and trust as a leader.

When staff members feel they're making a difference in the workplace, they are happier and more satisfied with their jobs. Open communication is very important to creating a cohesive work environment. When staff members feels comfortable approaching their supervisor or manager with an issue knowing it will be received without judgment or reprimand, a healthier workplace environment occurs naturally.

A leader is part of the solution. Trust is hard to regain once broken, so strong leaders make confidentiality a priority in order to build and maintain trust with their staff. When lines of communication remain open, others feel comfortable sharing their concerns.

Questions to Cover Building Trust Relationships in the Workplace:
1. Describe your current work relationship with your staff.
2. Describe your ideal workplace relationship with your staff.
3. How will improving your working relationships with others help you?
4. How will improving your working relationships with your staff make a difference?
5. What obstacles prevent you from improving these relationships?
6. What will you do to move past these barriers?
7. What are the benefits to making this work?
8. What action steps do you want to take?
9. Describe the workplace after achieving trusting relationships.

COACHING FOR PASSION TO SPARK PASSION IN OTHERS

Effective leaders are passionate about their work. Their passion can easily ignite excitement and creativity in the workplace. When leaders are enthusiastic about what they do, they inspire the same in others. Coaches can help clients identify their passion in the workplace. Asking your client powerful questions about what incites his passion can help him stir his passion!

> *"Asking your client powerful questions about what incites his passion can help him stir his passion!"*

Questions to Help Your Client Identify Their Passion:
1. What do you want from your work?
2. What do you like most about your career?
3. What do you want most from your profession?
4. What has given you the most gratification in your work?
5. What inspires passion for your work?
6. What is the perfect working day?
7. How do you describe your current level of decision-making and authority?
8. What do you want it to be?
9. How will you achieve what you want it to be?
10. In what areas do you receive the most positive feedback regarding your career?
11. What skills do you admire in others?
12. What skills do others admire in you?
13. What skills do successful people have?
14. What motivates you in your career?
15. What else will benefit you to be passionate about your career?
16. What specific action steps will you take to improve your level of motivation and excitement in your position?

COACHING CLIENTS TO GIVE AND ACCEPT HONEST FEEDBACK

Explore with your client/leaders the importance of providing honest feedback to their staff. Brainstorm how matters of performance are best addressed directly with individual staff members. Ask the client about speaking calmly with staff members about the areas that require improvement. Discuss with the client the possibility of receiving feedback from their staff members as well.

How does a coach open up this philosophy to a client/leader who isn't following this concept? Ask open-ended questions that probe towards honest feedback and self-reflection.

Questions that Probe for Honest Feedback and Self-Refection:
1. What application of feedback makes a good leader?
2. How open and honest is your staff with you?
3. How open and honest do you want your staff to be with you?
4. How will you support honest feedback?
5. How will you invite open and honest feedback with your staff?
6. How will you accept open and honest feedback from your staff?
7. What are the challenges you foresee of presenting open and honest feedback with your staff?
8. What are the benefits of honest feedback?

9. How will you implement this into practice in your workplace?

Good leaders are open to honest feedback and good suggestions, and truly effective leaders both listen and respond, then implement the suggestions and requests of others when appropriate.

WHAT IS A LEADER?

A leader is someone who is there for her staff. A leader listens with compassion and understanding, and assists whenever possible. She comes up with workplace solutions and evaluates how her decisions affect others. She is someone willing to stand out, stand up, and be part of solutions that help to achieve mutual goals. At times, a leader may be a mentor or a coach. She knows that being a leader can be a demanding and challenging job. Good leaders learn from their mistakes. Leaders use tools that enhance their awareness such as journaling or sitting in self-reflection. Some use lists to remember things. Other leaders invite input as a way to come up with solutions or new ideas.

When appropriate, good leaders seek help from a coach. Some hire coaches in areas they lack knowledge or expertise. Others hire coaches to grow and learn how to change habits to help them handle things differently in the future. Hiring a coach empowers the client/leader to discover ideas and solutions in areas of life and work with which they are challenged. This helps the client become aware of repetitive mistakes and begin to shift mindsets. Coaching helps client/leaders with strategies and solutions that can serve them throughout their careers.

> *"Coaching helps client/leaders with strategies and solutions that can serve them throughout their careers."*

BOUNDARIES FOR THE COACHING PROCESS

It is advisable that a coach/client relationship begin with a mutual understanding of a contractual coaching agreement and code of ethics. An agreed upon list of core values that guide the coaching process and provide boundaries for the relationship offer a useful set of guidelines for reference throughout the coaching relationship. It is valuable to have the code of ethics, core values, mission, and vision statement posted on the coach's website. To ensure good coaching practice it is important that the coach discusses with the client their expectations at the beginning of the relationship. The coach is not the client's friend; rather she is there to assist the client in moving forward with the client's aspirations and goals.

> *"To ensure good coaching practice it is important that the coach discusses with the client their expectations at the beginning of the relationship."*

COACHING GOOD BOUNDARIES AS THE KEY TO SUCCESSFUL LEADERSHIP

Coach your client to have healthy boundaries with members of his staff. Boundaries may be defined as the limits supervisors set for what are acceptable and unacceptable behaviors in the workplace. Ask your client to create their own guidelines and procedures regarding boundaries with their staff members. This will help the client to maintain appropriate behavior. When a subordinate crosses boundaries with his boss, he may exhibit an inappropriate attitude or fail to follow policy and procedures. Boundaries in the workplace create successful working relationships between supervisors and subordinates, and such boundaries can lead to a shared respect between the two.

Sometimes supervisors may incorrectly expect that their subordinates will automatically be loyal to them. Subordinates may do what is requested because they want to keep their jobs and/or want to please their boss, rather than act out of a sense of true loyalty. Successful leaders work to develop good rapport with each individual on their team. Though this may take some time and energy, it is well worth the effort in the long run.

Professional boundaries are essential to clearly identify the limits and responsibilities of everyone in the workplace. When workplace boundaries are specified, the organization works more efficiently, as each individual is accountable for his or her work performance, which makes the workplace a better, healthier environment for all involved.

> *"...each individual is accountable for his or her work performance, which makes the workplace a better, healthier environment for all involved."*

EXAMPLES OF APPROPRIATE AND INAPPROPRIATE BOUNDARIES

Here is an example of a supervisor with rigid boundaries: Chuck supervises a group of workers. When he converses with his staff he barks orders and has a negative demeanor. He doesn't ask the staff how the projects are going. Instead, he continuously looks for mistakes. He walks around with an angry scowl and is very unapproachable. He yells rather than speak in a normal voice and shouts from his desk for a staff member to come into his office instead of calling the person privately. He leaves the door open and degrades the staff about small nitpicky things. It is not unusual for a staff member to return to his or her desk feeling upset and useless. Others from the team feel sorry for that staff member but are reluctant, even afraid, to reach out and comfort in any way. One day, Neil, the Human Resource Department Director, walks past Chuck's office as he is yelling at a subordinate, and hears the way this supervisor is speaking. The following day, Chuck receives a notification to meet with Neil.

Neil recounts what he observed and informs Chuck that he is required to meet with a leadership coach to work on his leadership skills. Chuck is very angry and doesn't understand why he must meet with the coach, as he says that he has never needed it before. Neil registers Chuck for leadership classes immediately and informs Chuck that the process is mandatory or he will be asked to leave his supervisory position. Chuck storms out of Neil's office.

Here is an example of a supervisor with no boundaries: Cliff is very charismatic and upper management thinks he is on the rise. He invites specific staff members to join him at a bar after work and picks up the tab. Cliff has his favorites amongst the staff and occasionally allows them leave work early so they can join him at the bar. Cliff asks these specific staff members to do things they ordinarily would not do. Though they know what they are doing is wrong, they do what Cliff says because he is the boss. As time goes on, Cliff makes more and more unethical requests of his staff. When someone finally has the courage to say no to him, he humiliates and threatens that person and manipulates other staff members to turn against their co-worker. Because Cliff's subordinates fear for their jobs, they say nothing and put up with the abuse.

Here is an example of a supervisor with healthy boundaries: Amanda supervises a group of subordinates. She is consistently available to listen, support, and encourage her staff. As a good leader, she works with intention to build relationships of trust, accountability, and commitment with her staff members. Amanda empowers her team and supplies them with resources to succeed. She inspires her staff to pursue excellence in their work and encourages them in their personal goals as well. Amanda has a vision for her department and continually talks about that vision with others. She accepts and gives honest feedback, so her staff feels secure to discuss things with her freely. If one of her team members is struggling, she coaches them on improving his or her performance.

Amanda holds the philosophy that every person has something unique and special to offer to the team. She is very passionate about her job and stirs her staff to be passionate, as well. Amanda hires a leadership and life coach to empower her to continue moving towards her dreams and goals in life. She has a mentor and continues to attend training courses to increase her skills and knowledge.

Amanda schedules weekly one-on-one meetings with each member of her staff. This is an efficient time management tool, as the staff knows they have regular access to her and do not need to continually go to her with questions. She has asked each of them to write down their questions, suggestions, and concerns for the weekly meeting. By implementing these meetings Amanda is able to get her work done during regular work hours. Her staff understands that the weekly one-on-one time is for them so they are more apt to keep notes on what they want to discuss. When she meets with them, she gives them her undivided attention unless something urgent happens. Her staff members enjoy the opportunity to discuss their ideas, and Amanda coaches them during these individual sessions. These meetings establish boundaries and support work/life balance in Amanda's life and the lives of her staff, which naturally results is a healthy work atmosphere, where everyone has a sense of being heard and valued.

> *"Her staff members enjoy the opportunity to discuss their ideas, and Amanda coaches them during these individual sessions."*

Amanda has quarterly team meetings, wherein all staff members participate together. She invites her staff to put items for discussion on the meeting's agenda. Amanda begins with an inspirational moment, a quick team building exercise, and then moves through the agenda items. The meetings start and end on time. Everyone respectfully follows the rules of conduct of the meeting, which have been posted and agreed upon beforehand.

Amanda has provided her staff with journals to use to help with stress management and to generate new work ideas. She has encouraged everyone on her team to stop and take five minutes to journal their thoughts whenever they feel angry or stressed. She has assured them that their journals are private, and the contents are not shared unless someone chooses to share something he or she has written.

Questions to Help Your Client Establish Healthy Boundaries with Staff:
1. What is the purpose of setting boundaries with staff?
2. What are appropriate boundaries?
3. What are inappropriate boundaries?
4. What are the benefits of having boundaries?
5. How will you establish boundaries?
6. What are your action steps?

A LEADERSHIP COACH AND AN EXCELLENT LEADER HAVE SIMILAR CHARACTERISTICS

A coach and a leader have similar characteristics:
- Good listening skills
- Critical thinking skills
- Ability to communicate well by
- Asking open-ended questions
- Give constructive feedback
- Have excellent people skills
- Good time management skills
- Great facilitators
- Motivate others
- Great team building skills

- Dedicated and dependable
- Passionate about their job
- Lead by example
- Encourage others to accomplish their goals
- Hold others accountable for their actions and hold themselves accountable, as well
- Trustworthy, ethical and loyal

Just think, what are the possibilities if everyone followed these leadership qualities in the workplace? The creativity, passion, and job satisfaction easily create a well-balanced work environment.

Patti Oskvarek is a Certified Professional Coach through the Center for Coaching Certification and sole proprietor of Coaching for Inspiration with Patti. Her coaching niche areas include Personal, Business, and Leadership development. She provides to her clients over 20 years of supervisory, leadership, and government experience.

Patti became a professional coach to share her knowledge and expertise in leadership enrichment. She works with individuals and groups to become exceptional professionals and leaders. She coaches her clients with encouragement, support, positive reinforcement, confidence, accountability, and thought provoking questions to help them succeed.

Patti inspires others to pursue their passions in life. She is dedicated to helping others find passion, purpose, and confidence in all they do. Patti's mission is to encourage individuals and groups to enhance their personal and professional potential.

Patti lives in Arizona and in her free time she enjoys outdoor activities such as hiking, camping, taking photographs for her website and blog posts, as well as reading a good mystery novel.

www.CoachingforInspirationwithPatti.com

ATTENTION DEFICIT OR ATTENTION DIFFERENT?
Mikayla Phan

DIFFERENCES AND SIMILARITIES BETWEEN LIFE COACHING AND ADHD COACHING

The fundamental concept of coaching is that each of us has our own creativity, energy, and resources within, and the process of coaching empowers people to unlock their potential and maximize their quality of life. Although the coaching industry is relatively new to the world, this concept is not. Socrates, for example, had encouraged this same philosophy over 2000 years ago. Many eastern philosophies and religions, such as Buddhism, introduced this to civilizations even earlier, around the 6th century BC, specifically. I believe that in the rush towards materialism and modernity we globally have gotten lost in the shuffle of the fast-food mentality. Therefore, we have detrimentally shifted our gifts away from our inner souls.

> *"The fundamental concept of coaching is that each of us has our own creativity, energy, and resources within, and the process of coaching empowers people to unlock their potential and maximize their quality of life."*

It is only too ironic, then, that the quest for finding our inner strengths and the profession of coaching have emerged in the corporate setting, businesses large and small, as well as in government, education, and among individuals and families.

In point of fact, this quest has both emerged and taken hold like a wildfire in the driest conditions, thereby provoking the impact of coaching universally on an exponential level.

Certainly, there are targeted niches in which coaching seems to be in particular demand. For example, many Americans are becoming entrepreneurs and realize they have great ideas and are unsure of how to put them in action. They therefore seek coaches to help them make their career shift, create a business plan, and reach short and long term goals. In corporations, executives are recognizing while they pack a great product, they have weak links in their management skills or want help delegating multiple tasks efficiently to their employees and other team members. In education, coaching is slowly and surely becoming respected as essential. Teachers and principals understand the true differences between teaching, or instructing on an academic and intellectual level, and coaching on an intrapersonal level. Wherever the interests for coaching may exist, we are seeing the value and potency of the humanness, be it in any institution, congress, or in a family. For however much effort we put forth in making money hand over fist, manufacturing a new product, getting a promotion, or graduating summa cum laude, we also realize that it is only through the trust and balance of our humanity that we can achieve true success. Coaching taps into our humanity and empowers people to connect with their own inner gifts in order to succeed in life.

In other words, the demand for coaching has emerged in many different arenas all over the world. Life coaching, in particular, is one common type of coaching, perhaps because of the broad spectrum it can encompass. Unlike academic coaching or executive coaching, life coaching has a more open focus and therefore can be used for reaching several different goals across a wider market. Goals on which a person may want to focus in life coaching sessions can be a varied and broad range from exploring career options or changing a career path, planning a residential move, turning a hobby into a career, organizing a trip, creating an organized environment at work or home, meeting a deadline, prioritizing time for personal growth, to creating one's own vegetable garden. Theoretically speaking, as long as one has a goal, s/he is potentially interested in life coaching.

Because so many issues can be addressed in life coaching, there are niche areas within life coaching under which life coaches choose to specialize. Examples of these coaching niches include spirituality, nutrition, relationships, anger management, budgeting and finance, or legacy, to name a few. Because at least 10% of the American population alone is diagnosed with Attention Deficit, ADHD coaching has become a prominent type of life coaching.

There are minimal differences in the coaching method between most niches of life coaching. That said, ADHD coaching may very well be an anomaly because of the nature of ADHD itself. One result of ADHD is weakened executive function skills in the brain. Most of the necessary and foremost ingredients used to reach a goal require many or even all of the executive functions, such as prioritization, organization, planning, motivation, initiation, self-monitoring, working memory, and response inhibition. It is important to note that this does not mean one with weakened executive function skills is not capable of reaching goals nor eligible for coaching. On the contrary, due to the fundamental concept on which coaching is built, it is just as possible for individuals with weakened executive function skills to reach goals with the help of a coach as it is for people with highly developed executive function skills. It is the method by which ADHD coaching is approached that is different from that in life coaching.

> *"...it is just as possible for individuals with weakened executive function skills to reach goals with the help of a coach as it is for people with highly developed executive function skills."*

The International Coach Federation defines coaching as, *"partnering with clients in a thought-provoking and creative process that inspires them to maximize their personal and professional potential."* Professional coaches serve as a partner focused on empowering the clients to create the fulfilling results they want personally and/or professionally, thereby supporting clients to improve their performance and enhance their overall quality of life. It is true that as coaches, we are trained to fully listen, understand, and adjust our approach to each individual client so they discover their own solutions and strategies. In ADHD coaching, we tailor our approach even further.

ADHD coaching is a tailored collaborative partnership by which individuals are empowered to develop the awareness, cognitive processes, behavioral patterns, and environmental structures to overcome the performance deficits caused by weakened executive skills. Within the coach/client partnership, strengths, tools, talents, and innovative learning are explored and create successes, while simultaneously honoring the client as a creative and resourceful individual. Strategies and actions are designed together and progress is monitored by creating accountability in concert with goals. Therefore, ADHD coaching usually involves a tighter plan, more frequent sessions, and more accountability (check-ins) than in general life coaching.

> *"Within the coach/client partnership, strengths, tools, talents, and innovative learning are explored and create successes, while simultaneously honoring the client as a creative and resourceful individual."*

Both life coaching and ADHD coaching embrace the same ideals and core competencies, as well as honor the client as a creative and resourceful individual. Often ADHD coaches meet with clients at least once a week, sometimes daily, whereas other coaching programs may entail meetings which occur once or twice a month, or even once every couple of months.

AD/HD COACHING PRETEENS, TEENS, AND COLLEGE STUDENTS

Executive function skills start developing in the human brain during the first 6-12 months of life. However, because of the complexity of executive function skills, they continue to develop in stages well into adulthood. Due to the increasing demands in the world of academia, by the time we have reached adolescence we require a significantly developed range of executive function skills in order to effectively execute and perform tasks and solve problems. From activities as simple as getting up in the morning or remembering to take a homework assignment to school, to the complexity of regulating behavior in the face of temptations and distraction that will arise from the presence of peers, executive function skills are imperative to our success.

Let's be clear here. Because many of the complex executive function skills are developing during adolescence, teenagers in general will exhibit weak executive function skills to some extent, as this comes with the territory of being a teen and the lack of experience to practice their newly evolving executive function skills. For instance, the biological circadian rhythm, or "wake-sleep clock" in the adolescent body changes so that they don't become sleepy until somewhere between midnight and 2:00 AM, and therefore wake later because they still need a good night's sleep. Add to the mix the fact that school requires students to start classes anywhere between 7:30 AM and 8:30 AM, depending on the region of the US. With the addition of juggling extra-curricular activities, homework and due dates, and socializing, one gets a sense of the reasons most teens are frequently tired. In short, even teens with good executive function skills will struggle sometimes.

In preteens, teens, and college students with ADHD, the development of executive function skills are often delayed by up to 1/3 of their age and at least 2-3 years behind their true age. In other words, a 13 year old with ADHD could exhibit all the hormonal changes a teenager typically goes through physically, and at the same time have the organization, time-management, and impulse control skills of a nine or ten year old. Because it is usually around Middle School when the level of homework and expectations become heavier than in the earlier grades, this is the time when it is the easiest to see how weakened executive functions skills can cause obstacles for the individual with ADHD. That said, preteens and teens with ADHD too often are missing the help and assistance they need, perhaps because there is such an ambiguous line between weakened executive function skills in teens without ADHD and teens with ADHD.

I hear parents frequently say statements such as, "Well, Tommy is being a rebellious teen and just needs to manage his time better," or, "Well, Anna just needs to stop spending her time texting her friends and she'll be less inclined to be lazy and miss assignments." As a result, it is fortunate, indeed, when coaching is introduced to a preteen or teen with ADHD this early on; the earlier they can receive support during the time executive function skills are developing in the brain, the easier it will be for them to master these skills and learn how to work with their obstacles.

> *"...it is fortunate, indeed, when coaching is introduced to a preteen or teen with ADHD this early on..."*

Sadly, however, it is often not until individuals with ADHD reach college level that they experience their lives truly unraveling and therefore finally connect with a coach. Because it is usually this stage of life when it is the first time the student is truly independent from family physically and emotionally, weakened executive function skills can cause severe struggles for the college student. Even if the college student is in the same city or state, when living in a dorm or apartment s/he is still physically independent from the structure of home where parent(s) are in charge and probably took care of many of the necessary life skills such as cooking, cleaning, laundry, and even giving them their ADHD medication. While the college student (as does any teen) loves and wants the new independence, it can be very overwhelming to organize, prioritize, and initiate everything on one's own when the executive function skills may still be developing in the brain.

I think another difficult issue is social skills for college students at this point. Again, since this is the first time the college student may be truly independent, this also means in a social arena as well. Previous to college, people are socialized with the guidance of other adults, mostly their teachers and parents. There are play dates, group outings, and even when they are in high school often parents are still providing rides and other guidance to their teens on a social level.

In college there is limited supervision and guidance and teens are made to fend for themselves socially. When one of the weakened executive skills can be impulsivity, this can be a dangerous challenge to college students to juggle social time and study time. An added challenge is also the natural chemical process in the teen brain to try risky behavior as a natural way to declare independence in the world. If the teen also lacks proper impulse control, it can be disastrous.

After the teen years, individuals with ADHD can and do experience difficulty with executive function skills and benefit greatly from coaching. This is especially true for people who were without the positive assistance and resources earlier in their lives or during the teen years, or even for individuals who were diagnosed with ADHD after they were well into their adulthood.

LISTENING BUILDS TRUST IN THE COACHING PROCESS

In a general sense, we think of the concept of listening as the act of paying attention to someone or something in order to hear what is being conveyed. In contrast, as someone who has lived and learned the Chinese language and culture in Beijing for over a decade, as well as received a Bachelor's Degree in Chinese History, I think about the Chinese character for the word "listen". Unlike most Western languages, which are phonetically based, all Chinese characters are pictographs; each character represents a complete idea or thought. In the character for "listen", the symbol for "ear" is on the left side. On the right side is the concept of the individual, showing the symbols for "eyes", "undivided attention", and "heart". In other words, the word for "listen" indicates that true listening is achieved with much more than just the ears.

> *"In other words, the word for "listen" indicates that true listening is achieved with much more than just the ears."*

The Chinese were trying to tell us that active, or intentional, listening is done with all of our senses. It involves our ears (and both ears!), and also our eyes, conscious mind, and emotional connectivity. I believe that because the human brain is so complex and highly developed, we are very sophisticatedly equipped with the ability to multi-task. When I turn on my awareness to the kinds of things that I am able to pay attention to at any given time, I am almost shocked at how many things I actually am able to juggle. Because of this ability, and now reality in the fast-paced lives we have created for ourselves, we are multi-tasking and paying to attention to a myriad of things at one time—all the time.

On the one hand, this allows us to get more tasks done (answering an important call, signing an overdue document, calling the babysitter while driving to the bank), fulfill more needs for more people (cooking, finishing the laundry, and mediating the kids at the dinner table), and ultimately save time. Most of the time this works for us, and we successfully lead busy lives full to the brim with lots of activities, work, and play.

On the other hand, this can be a grave problem when we examine the art of true listening; for intentional listening requires all of our senses. The issue is not whether we can neuro-biologically use all our senses to listen to one thing, rather it is whether or not we can consciously stop multi-tasking with these senses as a force of habit and step outside of our comfort zone by shifting these senses to one task alone: listening to one person with our whole body.

"...intentional listening requires all of our senses."

So far, most people get by with listening with just their ears. What does this mean? This means that only the words being spoken by the one person is being entered into the ears of another person as sounds. Our brains translate those sounds into words and we cognitively categorize those words into information. This probably provides an explanation as to why unnecessary arguments turn into bitter fights, why people's feelings become hurt on accident from a variety of misunderstandings, or why deals are broken, and marriages end. For if humans were simple creatures, made of just data and information to be stored into other people's databases, then this "all ears" type of listening could work just fine! Because we are complex creatures with lots of grey areas in all aspects of our beings, it is impossible to actually listen properly without using our full awareness and all five senses.

> *"...it is impossible to actually listen properly without using our full awareness and all five senses."*

From the co-active coaching perspective, building relationships and developing intimacy and honesty with the client supports successful outcomes; active listening becomes one of the most important elements in the coaching process in order to facilitate this happening. Because it may be challenging for the ADHD client to articulate and express, both active listening coupled with reflective listening means the coach can discover a holistic picture of the client's objectives, as well as hear things between the lines.

THE CODE OF ETHICS SUPPORTS TRUST AND INTIMACY IN COACHING

Another important step in developing intimacy occurs in the beginning with the introduction to a Code of Ethics by the coach to the client and sponsor (if there is someone other than the client who is responsible for payment). Often times, a client knows for sure s/he wants to be coached and perhaps even may know some of the specific goals s/he wants to address in the coaching process. At the same time, the client may have some apprehension before coaching even begins, whether it is due to a difficulty in breaking the ice, the sensitivity to the stigma attached to having ADHD, and/or the process of hiring a coach. His or her own knowledge (or incorrect knowledge) about coaching and the coaching industry, concerns about trust and confidentiality issues, or even regarding legal concerns, especially if the coaching process is taking place within a large organization such as a corporation or business, are additional reasons.

Indeed, whenever there is a relationship about to be established between two parties, as in the coaching industry or profession, there is a certain level of apprehension that naturally exists because of the nature of the said relationship about to be formed: the client is going to identify an issue or roadblock that might be in the way of achieving his/her goal(s), and the coach is going to serve as a guide to the client as the client discovers the roadblocks and how to efficiently remove them. That's a fairly private and intimate thing to do! It is essential therefore, to establish a balanced and solid trust between the said parties. What better tool to establish trust could a Code of Ethics be?!

> *"It is essential therefore, to establish a balanced and solid trust between the said parties. What better tool to establish trust could a Code of Ethics be?!"*

A Code of Ethics is an important tool in the beginning of the client/coach relationship to provide a clear description of individual and social moral codes, as well as a Code of Conduct. Diversity within the human race means that we all may have a different set of moral codes in which we believe and follow. For this, it is supremely necessary for a certain set of moral codes to be specified and clearly understood between client and coach in case any could be in question.

Additionally, we live in a society where we have diversity among our species and also among our cultures on a global scale. Consequently, a Code of Ethics provides a bridge between different cultural practices, such as the tradition of gift giving. In more grave instances, there might be cultural areas of a different sensitivity, such as in many East Asian cultures where women's rights or ADHD is not recognized and the client may feel especially shy or distrustful and/or the sponsor or family members of the client may not feel the client needs coaching at all. Having a Code of Ethics which very clearly defines and explains that coaching is all about the client, supports the client to prioritize his/her own focus, and the client is empowered to discover and choose his/her own path, is the very kind of bridge it takes to establish trust from the beginning of the coaching relationship.

This prompts another important role of a Code of Ethics. A Code of Ethics is both important in establishing a trusting relationship between client and coach and also as a check-and-balance system for the involved parties. We see this when a conflict of interest arises. We might encounter potential relationships with clients who may pose a difficulty to us personally or professionally, for instance addressing goals within an issue which exceeds our skill level. Similarly, the topic on which a client might want to be coached may go against our own personal beliefs or moral code, such as divorce or adultery. Whatever the case, a Code of Ethics may help us assesses whether or not we can effectively coach the said client. Because the lines of distinction are so often very thin and ambiguous, a Code of Ethics can provide a way for coaches to determine whether or not there is a conflict of interest, and if so, how to address that specific conflict with the client/sponsor while still maintaining a professional and appropriate level of integrity.

A less sensitive role, and equally as critical, which a Code of Ethics provides is a set of clear boundaries in a general sense;

for example the nature of coaching and the coaching process. It also provides the client with specific and helpful details about the policies within the coaching relationship and process, continuation of coaching contract and relationship, and other related agreements that further support the trust and intimacy between client/sponsor and coach.

I had several insights from reviewing the Code of Ethics with regards to myself as a Life Coach specializing in ADHD Coaching. When working with individuals who have ADHD, the Code of Ethics is particularly important because one of the executive skills they struggle with is impulse-control. In addition, other weak and/or underdeveloped executive skills may include time management, emotional control, prioritization, and certain social skills. As a result, many people with ADHD are 2-3 years behind their peers in executive skills maturity. Having a clear Code of Ethics is paramount in the relationship between ADHD client and coach, for instance in the case of being on time for appointments or providing heightened accountability between and during sessions.

Furthermore, the role of a Code of Ethics between an ADHD client and myself as coach also provides a tangible first step in building a trusting relationship. This is especially critical because many people with ADHD have a difficult time trusting a professional who specializes in ADHD. In some instances, for example, it doesn't matter to the ADHD client that coaching is all about the client because h/she may already have had a terrible experience with someone else in a similar role, like a teacher, tutor, or even parent that may have made the client feel badly about him/herself, even if unintentional. People with ADHD have often been called lazy, irresponsible, stupid, naughty, or a whole host of other negative terms before they have even reached a coach's office. Therefore, it is only that much more important for a valued trust to be established. I think having a Code of Ethics is a wonderful way to begin forming that trust. It is a very objective thing between two subjective people (client and coach) and therefore is a great balance. In recognizing the diversity among the human race and between the cultures of our world, it is important to me that I use the Code of Ethics in all forms: online, in discussion, and in writing to accommodate visual, auditory, and kinesthetic

> *"In recognizing the diversity among the human race and between the cultures of our world, it is important to me that I use the Code of Ethics…"*

learners, and also to reiterate these Codes in various parts of the coaching relationship between my client and myself.

Because ADHD results in weakened executive functions, some of which include task initiation, prioritization, completing a task, and motivation, it is imperative for an ADHD coach to provide a means for the ADHD client to be accountable in the form of check-ins as well as be there at every step of the process, encouraging when things don't work and celebrating when there is success. A coaching contract, then, is also crucial in designing a partnership with the client because it provides a clear explanation of the coaching role, responsibilities, as well as the role and responsibilities of everyone else involved, i.e. the client and/or sponsor. It also details boundaries in the form of policies, such as how much I charge, how often we meet, when the payments are due, what to do if the client misses a session or is late. Most importantly, by stating these fundamentals in an open and honest fashion, this immediately starts building the foundation for a strong, trusting relationship within the coaching partnership between the coach and client.

People have suffered from ADHD for millennia; it was first written about by Scottish physician/author Sir Alexander Crichton in 1798 and was only described in detail more than 100 years later by English pediatrician, George Frederic Still, in 1902. ADHD has been very controversial as late as the 1970's and has only been given full recognition in mainstream society since the mid 1990's. As the research and knowledge of ADHD has come a long way, so too has the influx of coaching, primarily ADHD coaching. Regardless the age of the individual, even when the executive function skills are fully developed in the brain, we know that the ADHD brain itself beats to a different drum than the non-ADHD brain. The world is designed around the functionality of the non-ADHD brain and therefore people of all ages with ADHD can find it difficult to thrive in many facets of their lives. It is through the support of a coach that individuals with ADHD can discover and design new ways to succeed in a predominantly non-ADHD world. And, who knows? If we are able to open our minds to understanding the science of ADHD or the value and importance of coaching, then it is quite possible we are on our way to creating a world in which there are many different ways to thrive and be happy.

Mikayla Phan holds a Bachelor's degree from Kalamazoo College in Asian Studies with a concentration in Chinese History, and is fluent in Mandarin Chinese. She learned and lived the Chinese culture in Beijing for nine years.

Mikayla created and tailored her own home schooling curriculum for her son who has ADHD. She founded Beijing's only expatriate home schooling community group to date. In 2003, Mikayla wrote, "Path to Parenthood" which was published in a post-graduate textbook, *Beyond Cultural Anxieties: Ingredients of Fear, Tests of Character* (Trade Paperback, Sept 2004). Mikayla was the director of a children's program for which she trained the teachers and wrote a tri-level EFL curriculum.

Mikayla is a Certified Professional Coach and certified ADHD Coach, and has extensive experience coaching individuals with ADHD. Mikayla's writings have been featured on the Center of Coaching Certification website as a guest blogger.

Mikayla is establishing a bridge between ADHD and life skills learning through coaching and the creation of Phan Coaching Center. She and her teenage son reside in Madison, WI.

www.PhanCoaching.com

Coaching Thru Mental Health Challenges
Danielle Hark

I pride myself on being many things. I'm a coach, mentor, and advocate. I'm a photographer and writer. I'm a wife and mother. I'm also someone who has had to overcome mental health challenges throughout my life.

When I first learned about coaching years ago, I thought, *This all sounds nice, but I'm too broken to benefit from coaching, and I'm certainly too broken to be able to coach others.* Then I learned through my training and experience, both coaching and being coached, that I benefit hugely from coaching and am a highly effective coach to others.

In the following pages, I will explore the ways in which coaches can effectively work with individuals with mental health challenges. I will also address the ways in which we, as coaches, can effectively coach others while dealing with our own personal challenges.

Part I: Coaching Individuals with Mental Health Challenges

Some coaches believe an individual must be whole and healthy to benefit from coaching, and are averse to working with people who have mental health challenges.   I embrace the opportunity.

One in four adults suffers from a mental illness in a given year. This represents a huge part of the population that will benefit from coaching if we expand our mindsets and practices. I believe we all could be perceived as less than whole at one time or another, whether that is from stress at home or work, situational anxiety, or depression from a loss or tough times. Does that mean that we can't benefit from coaching at those times? Of course we benefit in those times! Anyone can benefit from coaching. The technique and conduct is adjusted from time to time to match the place where the client is at in that given moment, just as we adjust to different personality types and learning styles.

THERAPIST, PSYCHIATRIST, OR COACH?

Throughout my life, I have been to psychiatrists, therapists, and life coaches. I know firsthand the power of each. An individual who has mental health challenges can benefit from seeing more than one type of mental health professional, because their specialties are so different. Coaching can successfully occur concurrently with treatment by a mental health professional, and does not replace it.

According to Meg Buck, a certified life coach in practice in New

Jersey and Pennsylvania since 2005, "Coaching and therapy are different animals. There are some aspects of coaching that are related to therapy, such as identifying and resolving current obstacles in order to move forward, but therapy helps a patient work through a spectrum of issues, both past and present, while coaching is all about the future."

Here is a breakdown of different types of professionals that can be of assistance to a person with mental health challenges. You will see that the roles vary greatly.

Psychiatrists (M.D., D.O.) are medical doctors specializing in diagnosing and treating mental illness. A psychiatrist is a licensed physician who completed a residency in psychiatry through a program approved by the American Medical Association or the American Osteopathic Association. Psychiatrists can prescribe medication as well as engage in psychotherapy.

Psychologists (Ph.D., Psy.D. or Ed.D) are individuals with a doctorate in psychology who are in practice as a clinical or counseling psychologist.

Social Workers (MSW) have master's degrees in social work. They are trained in psychotherapy and social work techniques.

Psychologists, social workers, counselors, and therapists utilize psychotherapy, as well as some psychiatrists. Therapy is a technique used to explore the past and present. It is a helpful tool for the assessment and treatment of psychological disorders.

Laura Alper, a clinical social worker who has practiced for over 30 years, explains, "Psychotherapy often reaches into the past helping the client identify the themes, feelings, and behaviors, that have undermined the client's successful movement through life stages. Understanding these life themes can liberate the client from stuck-ness by sharpening awareness of emotional traps and by expanding a repertoire of behavioral skills, which facilitate more successful life choices. From this conscious vantage point, the new psychological toolbox then dovetails beautifully with the skills being developed in a coaching relationship."

Life Coaches focus on the present and the future. They help a person to see where he or she is at currently in relation to where they want to be. The coach supports and encourages the client as they implement changes and work towards the personal goals they have created. A coach encourages a client to think and discover things for themselves, as opposed to giving advice.

> *"Life Coaches focus on the present and the future."*

An individual who is seeing a therapist and/or psychiatrist for assessment, analysis, and/or medication will also benefit from seeing a life coach who will help him or her set goals and take action steps towards achieving those goals. According to Buck, "Coaching and therapy together can be a phenomenal winning formula for people dealing with mental health issues. You can create a new path for yourself [through coaching] while finding a way to complete the old one [through therapy]. Perhaps one of these in fact might lead to the other." It works best when the client's mental health professional and coach are in contact, so that both can have an even bigger picture from which to work and best support the client.

> *"An individual who is seeing a therapist and/or psychiatrist for assessment, analysis, and/or medication will also benefit from seeing a life coach who will help him or her set goals and take action steps towards achieving those goals."*

CONDUCT FOR COACHING INDIVIDUALS WITH MENTAL HEALTH CHALLENGES

It is important when seeing someone who has a history of mental health challenges or is experiencing them when they come in to establish very clear ground rules from session one.

1. Boundaries

Coaching is unregulated at this time and thus there is no singular code of ethics or boundaries. It is highly important to become a member and adopt a code of ethics from a reputable source, such as the International Coach Federation, so that standards of professional conduct are clear to everyone involved. This code of ethics is ideally then posted on your web site or given to the client to review during the introductory meeting.

Some boundary and conduct issues are relatively cut and dry. For instance, a coach may not become sexually intimate with a current client. When it comes to friendship, it is a bit more complicated and may not be laid out word for word in a code of ethics. In this case the boundaries are essential so that the coaching relationship stays fully focused on the client and that it not be impaired by other considerations.

It is important to build a rapport with each client and to establish a foundation of trust, understanding, and respect. Professional coaches are friendly with clients, without crossing too far over the friendship line. This is not as steadfast a rule for coaches as for other mental health professionals; it is important, especially when dealing with clients with mental health challenges who may already be struggling with boundary issues. If you cross too far, you are prone to becoming affected by the choices that the client is taking. You learn about their past and outside factors that take you away from focusing on the present moment and the future. You also are more likely to advise and take on a mentoring role instead of strictly adhering to your role as coach.

"Boundaries are exceptionally important for a coach," Buck says, "Coaches typically are empathetic people and it's important that we don't become attached to or involved in our clients' issues. This is not always easy, but a highly trained coach is able to thoroughly remove him- or herself from the equation. The gravity of remaining removed goes beyond not getting pulled in to a client's world; utmost, we must remain impartial in order to provide the best coaching we can. Only an outsider can thoroughly observe and recognize behavioral obstacles or detrimental thought patterns."

It can help to set boundaries about emails and calls between sessions. Occasionally there are situations that come up that require immediate attention. That said, ensure the client is aware if between sessions contact must be kept to a minimum. If calls require more than a set amount of time, say 15 minutes, it will be considered a session and the coach is to be compensated for such. These social boundaries are especially important when coaching individuals with personality or mood disorders who may be seeking validation and attention beyond the traditional coach-client relationship.

2. Empathy

It is important to utilize active listening skills during sessions, and to convey warmth, sympathy, and at times empathy, so that the client knows that you are really listening to them and understanding them. Some coaches choose to disclose things about themselves to their clients when situations arise with which they can empathize. This can be helpful, as long as it is strictly in the best interest of the client, and the focus stays on the client and not the coach.

Buck suggests, "For the most part a coach shouldn't offer up personal information during sessions; however instances do arise where a personal anecdote might help rather than hinder. Be succinct. The client doesn't need your details. Focus on the breakthrough giving only enough background to relate, and then immediately bring the conversation back to the client. Let the client gain insight from your story--do not provide it for them."

Recovery coaches, for instance, often reveal that they too are in recovery so that the client feels understood. Such a reveal can be incredibly helpful for the client as long as it remains clear that the coach is not a sponsor or mentor. Such a shift in the relationship would compromise the coaching process.

Remember, a coaching relationship is a professional relationship. It is possible to create a professional friendship as long as boundaries are clear and consistent.

It is also possible to coach someone who is an existing friend or acquaintance; it is even more important to discuss the ground rules before you start, and what is and is not appropriate. Confidentiality is a must, as is leaving friendly discussions at the door. Discussing situations about which you are privy because of the friendship can interfere with keeping proper coach conduct. These conversations can prevent the focus from being fully on the future and creating goals and paths leading to those goals.

3. Compliance

One of the elements of the International Coaching Federation Code of Ethics states: "I will suggest my client seek the service of other professionals when deemed necessary or appropriate." This is a big one when you are working with clients with mental health challenges. A client must know that if upon a professional assessment or at any time during the coaching process the coach believes that a client is best served to seek additional help, he or she will be referred to another kind of professional. If in the introductory session a client expresses that they are coming in to seek relief from psychological or emotional pain, they will be referred to a therapist. The same goes if trauma or adverse past issues come up, or if there is fear that the client may be harmful to themselves or others. If medical or medication issues come up, they will be referred to a psychiatrist or other medical professional.

Just because a client is being referred to another mental health professional does not mean that the coaching process must be terminated. It does mean that the client must agree to be compliant in order to proceed. It means that he or she must see the doctor or therapist, or someone with the appropriate training. Often the individual will sign a release so that the doctor(s) and coach together can determine how to best coordinate and support them in the respective processes.

> *"Just because a client is being referred to another mental health professional does not mean that the coaching process must be terminated."*

PART II: COACHING THROUGH MENTAL HEALTH CHALLENGES

Everyone experiences mental health challenges at one time or another. It's important that we, as coaches, continually self-assess to make sure we are able to be the best coach we can be for each client. They deserve our best.

As Alper says, "The first step in caring for others is to invest in your own self-care."

Self-care and assessment are essential on an ongoing basis, before, during, and in the time between coaching sessions.

> *"Self-care and assessment are essential on an ongoing basis, before, during, and in the time between coaching sessions."*

BEFORE A SESSION

It's important to assess your mood and emotional state before each session. If you gauge yourself as anything other than open, balanced, and present, create a pre-session routine that will help you find that place. Think of it as a toolbox that contains calming and relaxing tools, just for you. These are ways to get out of your mind, and into the present moment, for your client and for you.

> *"If you gauge yourself as anything other than open, balanced, and present, create a pre-session routine that will help you find that place."*

Here are some helpful tools and techniques to add to your pre-session routine. Add them to your mental toolbox or create an actual box from which you can grab something calming and grounding as needed.

Stretching – Stress restricts blood flow causing your muscles to tense up, especially the muscles in your back, neck, and shoulders. People who sit for long periods of time, such as coaches, are especially prone to such muscle tension. Stretching can help release the tension, which can in turn reduce your stress. Taking five minutes between clients to stretch your upper back, lower back, neck, and shoulders can also reduce pain, increase circulation, improve your posture, and make you more mindful of your body.

Getting Outside – Take a few minutes to walk in nature, or at least take a stroll around the block to get some sun and fresh air. Pay special attention to your surroundings... the sound of leaves crunching, the different textures under your feet, the colors, and the smells. Your body movement, the change of environment, and the Vitamin D can all give you a boost and allow you a fresh start when you go back into your coaching space.

Meditation – Meditating can be a powerful transition practice. There are different practices of meditation that work for different people. There are walking meditations, sound meditations, or visual meditations. You can get an app or a guided meditation if it helps to focus on someone else's voice, or you can record your own. Alper, a meditation instructor and practitioner who completed Harvard's mind-body institute and studied meditation and Buddhist psychology, recommends a Buddhist meditation practice called Metta (the application of love to suffering). The instruction is, while seated in a comfortable position with eyes closed, to first direct healing thoughts towards yourself and then extend them to others. Even dedicating ten or twenty minutes of meditation, three times per week, is incredibly helpful for stress reduction.

Engaging your senses – One way to quickly bring yourself back to the present moment is by using your senses. You can light a candle with a relaxing scent, apply lotion with calming herbs such as lavender, listen to music, and/or enjoy a soothing cup of tea. The warmth and scent are very grounding.

Creativity – This is my favorite tool because I love taking photos (even with my phone). Creativity can be anything from coloring on a post-it note to making a collage on the pages of an old book to making a mandala out of sticks and rocks. Creativity is a fun tool for self-expression, in addition to being a way to relax and refocus between clients.

> *"Creativity is a fun tool for self-expression, in addition to being a way to relax and refocus between clients."*

Affirmation – Some coaches use affirmations with their clients and not for themselves. Do it. Affirmations are powerful tools of transformation that take only a few minutes of your time at most. Using affirmations will shift the way you think, feel, and even speak. These simple statements have within them the ability to shift your mindset to a more positive place and spark feelings of confidence that lead to positive action and meaningful change for yourself and your clients.

Gratitude – Think about all of the things for which you are thankful. Write down at least one thing each day. You can put them in a jar or a journal. Then during moments when you want a quick boost, you will have a bountiful reminder of wonderful things in your life to be thankful for on that day, and every day.

DURING A SESSION

Be aware of triggers – Working with clients who have similar issues to your own can be triggering and possibly even dangerous, so it is essential to keep tabs on yourself, take care of yourself, and get support or help when appropriate.

During a session, be aware when thoughts, feelings, or judgments come up, and set them aside to process later. Letting them affect you interferes with your ability to coach, and it can lead to your own relapse. You must stay present for your client and yourself.

According to Alper, "If you become triggered due to the client's issue within a session, it is imperative to use the tools of your own recovery to effectively differentiate the client's struggles from your own. It is possible to mindfully observe the urge to react, without actually reacting. From a place of neutral observation, the coach can continue to be present."

One way to do so is by utilizing mindfulness techniques.

Mindfulness - While having its roots in Eastern Buddhist practices, Mindfulness has become common practice in Western psychology. If you are being mindful, you are not ruminating on the past or worrying about the future, which allows you to focus fully on your client.

Mindfulness helps both your mind and body. It lowers stress levels, and it helps your memory and focus, allowing you to tune out distractions.

> *"Mindfulness helps both your mind and body."*

Mindfulness is a meditative practice, and it is also a living life practice. Anything can be done mindfully... eating, brushing your teeth, walking, and yes, even coaching. How? Observe, notice each breath, feel your bodily sensations, and allow thoughts, feelings, and emotions to come and go with open acceptance.

"A coach who is sufficiently removed can be both empathetic and protected," Buck adds. This takes practice. Rarely is one able to coach on a close-to-home topic for the first time without being affected. With practice, we build up a tolerance for such triggers and can coach from an emotional distance."

If you find yourself feeling triggered, take a moment to breathe and mindfully ground yourself in the present, and then use the open-ended questions to maintain a fully client-centered session.

AFTER A SESSION

During the time between sessions, be sure you are taking care of yourself and regularly seeing doctors to keep balance of mind and body. You are the best coach when you are in top form, mentally and physically.

Take Care of Your Body – Eat well. Create and maintain healthy habits. See doctors as appropriate and follow their instructions. Being healthy supports a healthy mind.

Get Active – Exercise and movement help minimize depression and anxiety. Exercise releases chemicals in your brain which help you feel better. You can go for a hike, play sports, play games with your kids, or even garden. Find a way to get active that you enjoy and do it.

Creativity – There are many ways to get creative. You can engage in art whether that is painting, coloring, or taking photos. You can also experiment with other creative activities such as knitting, cooking, or baking. The key is not what you create, it is that you create. It's about being in the present moment and enjoying the process of creating.

Help Other People – Helping other people helps you too. It gives you the experience of accomplishing great things and is satisfying. Helping others is a positive way to connect too.

Nature – Get out of your home or office and into nature. You can sit and meditate, read a book, or just bask in the soothing sights, sounds, and smells of nature. Even a few minutes in nature can help you push the reset button.

Sleep – Lack of sleep can increase your chance of getting depressed, or make existing depression worse. It can also increase anxiety and irritability. Sleep deprivation causes fatigue that makes it harder to exercise and take care of yourself. Make sure to get those crucial zzzzzz's to help your mood, as well as immunity, memory, and overall functioning. Consider listening to your recorded affirmations, adding white noise, warm caffeine-free drinks, turning off the screens in the bedroom, and refraining from eating before bed. Keep a bedtime routine, which can be similar to your pre-session routine in that it incorporates things that are calming to you.

In closing, through engaging in self-assessment and self-care before, during, and after sessions, we will be highly effective coaches, even when we are experiencing personal challenges.

We will also naturally succeed in coaching people with mental health challenges by maintaining a clear code of conduct, boundaries, and friendly, professional empathy.

We have the opportunity to help people who are struggling with their mental health to be able to focus on the present, figure out attainable goals, and move forward towards those goals in a meaningful and positive way. We, as coaches, can empower people with mental health challenges who feel lost and broken, and help them to help themselves expand and move forward.

Danielle Hark is a wellness writer, professional photographer, and freelance photo editor with work featured in the Huffington Post, Psychology Today, Dr. Oz's YouBeauty, Working Mother, Beliefnet, and Family Circle Magazine.

Danielle is a mental health advocate. She is the founder and director of Broken Light Collective, a non-profit enhancing the lives of people living with or affected by mental illness. Broken Light Collective provides opportunities to share photographic work in supportive environments, raises awareness and fights stigma through art, education, advocacy, and outreach.

Danielle is expanding into the role of Certified Professional Coach in the areas of mental health, wellness, and creativity. As someone who has personally been affected by mental health challenges herself and with people she loves, she is especially attuned to the sensitive needs of her clients. She enjoys working with people who are stuck on creative projects as well as people who want to get in touch with their creative selves.

Danielle lives, creates, and coaches with her husband and favorite models, her young daughter and shelter pup.

www.DanielleHark.com

COACHING PARENTS OF TEENS
Karen Wrolson

PARENTING - A CHALLENGING JOB

Parenting is at its most difficult during the children's teen years. The parenting style that used to work quite well when they were in their younger years suddenly isn't working anymore. The teenagers don't even acknowledge the word "no", rules are ignored and even flaunted, and previously effective consequences don't seem to have any impact.

In addition, the closeness between the parent and child that used to be is different or even gone. The teen may filter or stop sharing feelings with mom and dad and become sullen – sometimes even bursting into bouts of screaming and/or abusive language. Hour after hour is spent behind their bedroom door, and only after pressure do they begrudgingly come out to eat.

Oftentimes parents feel bewilderment, as it seems their teenaged child is changing into someone else. Commonly you will hear these parents exclaim, "I never know what he is going to do anymore!" "She has changed so much. I feel like I don't even know her." "Where is that sweet boy I raised? Now he is always so sullen. I worry about how unhappy he seems to be."

Parents experience an overwhelming roller coaster of emotions:

desire to be close to their child, sadness as overtures are rebuffed, shock as their teenager flies out the front door despite the order to stay home, anger eventually becoming fear as the hours tick by and the child has not yet returned home, shame when called to the principal's office for yet another incident. Instead of enjoying the last few years their child will be under their roof, parents simply try to endure and begin to look forward to the day the teen moves out.

PARENT COACHES – PREPARATION BEFORE COACHING

Parents may seek out the assistance of parent coaches.

Please note: when using the term 'parent coach' I am referring to those who have had training and who have also earned a certification in coaching. I do not consider anyone a parent coach if they have not had proper training. Simply having been a parent does not qualify someone to be a parent coach. Using myself as an example, even after more than twenty years of being a Master's Level Counselor, I did not consider myself a coach until I had undergone training and become a certified coach. There are specific coaching skill sets attainable only through training, (preferably International Coach Federation approved programs) that are necessary for coaching.

> *"Simply having been a parent does not qualify someone to be a parent coach."*

If you are a parent coach, I strongly suggest you educate yourself about the following two areas:
- Developmental changes in the teen years (physically, cognitively, and social-emotionally)
- Parenting modifications necessary to meet the changing needs of teens

In this chapter I will provide some rudimentary information in those two areas. Please take note: what I am providing is simplified – intended for a general overview. I encourage you to do more reading on these two topics as part of your preparation.

DEVELOPMENTAL STAGES OF ADOLESCENCE

When I work with young people and/or their parents, I often reflect upon my own teenager years. I remember a tremendous range of emotions – from feeling elated with happiness to bouts of depression. The emotions could switch from day to day. I can still hear my mother asking me, "Well, what would make you happy?" I also remember responding many times with, "I don't know!" Those years were confusing to myself and to my parents. I know I certainly would not want to repeat them. So, I begin my work with this population by remembering that this is, by nature, a difficult period for everyone.

"...this is, by nature, a difficult period for everyone."

A great deal of the discomfort for both parents and teenagers stems from the powerful developmental stages the young people are moving through. As parent coaches, we and our clients will benefit from a good understanding of the progression of transformation. Let's begin now with a general overview of the physical stages, followed by the cognitive changes, and then conclude with the social/emotional developmental stages. As you consider how all these changes simultaneously occur, you will agree it makes sense that teens seem confused and frustrated.

PHYSICAL DEVELOPMENT OF TEENS

Early Adolescence: Puberty 11-13 years (approximate)
- Growth of body hair, increase in oil production in hair/skin
- Increase of perspiration
- Physical growth – weight and height
- Girls – menstruation, breast and hip development
- Boys – deepening of voice, wet dreams, growth in testicles and penis
- Sexual interest increases

Middle Adolescence: 14-18 years (approximate)
- Physical growth slows for girls
- Physical growth continues for boys
- Puberty is complete

Late Adolescence: 19-21 years (approximate)
- Women tend to be fully developed
- Men may continue to add body hair, height and weight, muscle mass

Significant issues regarding physical development:
- Teens develop at different rates
- Girls who mature faster may feel self-conscious due to teasing (parents of these girls may want to explore teaching them about respect and limits)
- Boys who do not develop muscle mass similar to their peers often feel embarrassed
- Some girls develop eating disorders at this stage due to a natural increase in body fat
- A healthy diet, exercise, and adequate sleep will help avoid medical problems while also contributing to a healthy self-image

COGNITIVE DEVELOPMENT OF TEENS

Early Adolescence: 11-13 years (approximate)
- Focus is on the present, with few thoughts about their future
- Burgeoning interest in morals - what is right and wrong
- Beginning to think abstractly
- More interest in learning

Middle Adolescence: 14-18 years (approximate)
- Increasing capacity for abstract thinking
- Thinking about the meaning of life
- Able to set goals
- Interested in moral reasoning

Late Adolescence: 19-21 years (approximate)
- Able to delay gratification
- More concern about the future
- Can think ideas through
- Begin to examine inner feelings
- Continue to be interested in moral reasoning

Significant issues regarding cognitive development:
- They are beginning to struggle with the meaning of their life
- They benefit from someone with whom they can process the inner feelings they are focused on
- Teens are beginning to question the values others have taught them (explore with parents how this is a natural part of teen cognitive development)
- Teens deal with almost daily pressures and choice making while they are still trying to determine what they feel is right and wrong
- Exposure to negative influencers (violent games, movies, music, etc.) will have a deep impact upon their developing sense of right and wrong

BRAIN DEVELOPMENT OF TEENS

- Frontal lobes of the brain, which control impulsivity and decision making, are not fully developed until age 25
- Reactions and emotions come from the Amygdala area of the brain, which matures earlier than the frontal lobes.

Significant issues regarding brain development:
- Teens react quicker and more forcefully with limited control from the undeveloped frontal lobes

SOCIAL-EMOTIONAL DEVELOPMENT OF TEENS

Early Adolescence: 11-13 years (approximate)
- Moodiness, more conflict with parents
- Desire for more privacy
- Begin to test rules
- More influenced by peer group
- Increased awkwardness and worry about not fitting in
- Desire for independence begins
- Begin to question parent's decisions

Middle Adolescence: 14-18 years (approximate)
- Egocentric
- Range from excitement about their life to depression and lack of hope

- Distance themselves – want greater independence
- Stronger desire for friendships
- Rely on friends when decision making
- Strong desire to be popular
- Begin to feel love and passion
- Concern about changing bodies

Late Adolescence: 19-21 years (approximate)
- Display greater concern for others, less self-involved
- Begin to develop serious relationships
- More self-reliant
- Better sense of identity
- More emotionally stable

Significant issues regarding social-emotional development:
- They often begin to question parents' credibility
- They have anxieties about popularity and their changing bodies
- They have a desire for relationships
- Distancing themselves from parents is natural and is separate from their feelings for their parents

PARENTING DEVELOPMENT IN RESPONSE TO ADOLESCENT DEVELOPMENT

Since young people change so much between the years of 11 and

21, parents are called upon to change the way that they parent. In this section I will help you, the coach, understand how to support parental methods developing in response to adolescent changes.

PARENTING METHODS FOR THE 11-13 YEAR OLD

Let's first take a look at early adolescence, which typically occurs between the years of 11 and 13. As a reminder from the previous information on developmental stages, this young person is undergoing a significant amount of physical changes. They become more interested in sexuality due to their bodies maturing. They do not think about the future and act impulsively due to the immaturity of their brain – especially in the frontal lobes, which are responsible for control in decision-making. They are starting to realize there are different perspectives on what is right and what is wrong.

They become moody and may begin to engage in conflict with their parents – at a minimum questioning parental decisions and at a maximum rebelling against parental control. Their peers are becoming more significant to them and they worry excessively about fitting in.

The early adolescent wants explanations from their parents so strategizing how to engage in discussions with their child is beneficial. Simply saying "no" will no longer suffice. Explore how to effectively invite and listen to their child's opinions. Ask about their openness to negotiating the rules to allow increasing responsibility and privileges based upon responsible behavior at decreasing levels of restrictions.

> *"Explore how to effectively invite and listen to their child's opinions."*

Ask your parent clients how they will create opportunities to speak about their child's physical development. Explore their options to help their children understand that their bodies may be developing slower or faster than their peers, and that eventually everything will even out. In light of their interest in their sexuality, now is also the time for parents to teach the youth about self-respect and the establishment of boundaries for their protection.

Prepare with parents to initiate discussions about morality beginning with the years of 11-13. Note the word choice of 'discussions' instead of 'lectures'. Parents can utilize television shows or current events as discussion springboards, inviting their children's opinions. Lyrics to popular music are also effective conversation starters. Lyrics reflecting hatred of police or violence towards women typically result in a lively discussion. The parent will want to be careful not to reflect a generalized hatred of complete genres like rap music as this will typically result in the teenager becoming defensive. The youngsters will be quick to point out that 'not all rap is bad'. In fact, the wise parent acknowledges that there are some good messages within that genre while displaying a concern over particular songs or messages. I have found it very effective for parents to be willing to sit and listen to their children's music with them. While it is unnecessary to proclaim a new appreciation for the music, it is helpful to acknowledge that music which is not offensive.

Normally these young people are beginning to desire privacy. This is completely normal and the parents will want to strategize ensuring a balance with the amount of time on activities the child finds fascinating while at the same time worry the parents. Often children spend 4-6 hours weekday evenings and full weekend days on computer games or in chat rooms! Exploring limits on computer and phone usage is important. One option for parents is to invite the youngster to be a part of establishing these limits. Empower the parents to negotiate built-in rewards for compliance.

PARENTING METHODS FOR THE 14-18 YEAR OLD

A review from our previous information on this developmental period indicates that young people's physical changes are slowing down. They are developing the capability to set goals for themselves and of thinking about the future. They begin to question the meaning of life.

They tend to be egocentric and focused on their own feelings, which now include love and passion. They seek advice from their friends while ignoring the admonitions of their 'archaic' parents. They become more distant from their parents due to their desire for independence. This may result in loud arguments and violations of family rules. They can be excessively moody during these years.

When I work with parents, I ask them about their interests in their child becoming independent. We talk about ways in which they can foster this growth while still providing a safety net. I ask parents about holding open discussions with their children regarding the family rules and their child's feelings and concerns. As a family unit they can construct new rules. Empowering the adolescent to have input in this process helps them feel respected as an individual. Walk through each suggested change by extending out the possible ramifications of each modification. This helps them practice thinking ahead.

> *"Empowering the adolescent to have input in this process helps them feel respected as an individual."*

This young adult that has an active part in determining consequences and rewards for following the new rules has ownership. Parents are often amazed at how much better their children behave when their children have buy-in to the new rules as a result of being engaged with the negotiation. It can be difficult for parents to consider changing their rules and expectations. I ask these questions: "What are the unacceptable risks in making changes?" and "What are the benefits of engaging your child in negotiating changes?"

For example, let's say the adolescent wants a later curfew. I help the parent prepare statements and questions that will lead to a discussion in which they determine a mutually satisfactory adjustment, complete with resulting privileges and consequences. They may agree to extend the curfew by 30 minutes if at the same time they ask the child, "What will you guarantee to me if it is extended?" Often the young person comes up with some great ideas like, "I will call you every hour and tell you where I am." Possibly also, "If I am late once, then I return to my old curfew for one week." The parent may also counter with, "Well, that means you are away from home an additional 2.5 hours every week. In that case, I want you to promise me that you will be with us for every family dinner." Or, "Well, then I want you to promise that you will be with the family for our Sunday night pizza and game night every week."

PARENTING METHODS FOR THE 19-21 YEAR OLD

The storm often begins to calm as youngsters reach this age.

They are beginning to develop better control over their impulses and are starting to plan for their future. Their emotions tend to be better regulated. They are developing the ability to look outside themselves and experience concern for others.

This is a wonderful time for parents to engage in meaningful discussions. Help your parents discover springboards for discussions along with the importance of being open about their own frustrations, fears, and joys. Also, explore the balance between talking and listening! One common goal that works is to listen to understand instead of listening to refute and challenge. Explore resources about active listening and communicating effectively.

> *"Also, explore the balance between talking and listening!"*

Since these young people are very interested in life after high school, parents have an opportunity to help them explore their options. For example, driving them to potential educational/training facilities is a fun time for all. Helping them seek out better employment options is something they will appreciate. Explore with your parents how they express being excited for their children and display eagerness to help them brainstorm their future. Ask parents how they will ensure their young adult makes their own choice instead of acquiescing to or complying with parental preferences. In some cases it is a good time for parents to share examples of mistakes they made at this age. This means the parents are more approachable as they help their youth understand errors are inevitable and can be learned from.

PARENT COACHING SESSION GUIDELINES

Now that you have a basic understanding of adolescent development along with responsive parenting methods, you have a good platform from which to begin your coaching of parents. If you also serve as your client's educator in these areas be clear when you are in a teaching mode and when you are in the coaching role. Following are suggestions regarding your first, second, and ensuing coaching sessions.

> *"If you also serve as your client's educator in these areas be clear when you are in a teaching mode and when you are in the coaching role."*

FIRST COACHING SESSION

During this first session, your role is to develop a complete picture of how your client is doing in a variety of areas. Explain to your client that some of the questions may seem to pertain to areas outside of parenting and at the same time are significant for understanding all of the influencing factors in their lives. Advise them that this session is typically longer than the standard one hour. Also, let them know you will be taking notes in order to assist them. Assure them that your focus will be on them while you are writing. Encourage them to be in an environment that is quiet, comfortable, and ensures their full attention is on the conversation. Phones, computers, and televisions are off. Others in the vicinity are notified that they are in a meeting.

> *"Encourage them to be in an environment that is quiet, comfortable, and ensures their full attention is on the conversation."*

Here is the sequence I find helpful in my coaching with parents:

Who are your family members? What are their ages?

For each family member named, ask the following:
    a) How do you describe the general quality of your relationship with this person?
    b) What are you happy about in this relationship?
    c) What are some areas you want improved?

What are your goal(s) for each relationship?

Describe the culture of your family. Elaborate on the following:
    a) Amount of time spent as a family
    b) Rate the quality of the time together
    c) Family activities inside and outside the home
    d) Family eating habits
    e) Typical weeknights and typical weekends

  f) Summers and vacations
  g) Privacy afforded to each member
  h) Primary decision making method for each person
  i) Expectations of each family member
  j) Rate communication between each member
  k) How is affection expressed?
  l) Discipline methods (consequences & rewards)
  m) Rules and limits

What are your goals regarding your family's culture?

What are the health habits of the family?
  a) Eating routine
  b) Exercise
  c) Personal care

What are your goals for your family's health?

Share information on each family member's life outside of the home:
  a) Career
  b) Education
  c) Free time activities
  d) Community involvement
  e) Friends

What are your goals for supporting each family member's life outside of the home?

What will your family be like after reaching your goals? Describe fully using senses of seeing, hearing, and

feeling plus maybe even smelling and tasting.
- a) Emotionally
- b) Physically
- c) Spiritually

What could prevent you from reaching these goals?

How will you move past these challenges?

What resources do you have to help achieve your goals?

How do you want me (the coach) to help keep you accountable?

SECOND COACHING SESSION

You now have a sense of the areas of concern as well as your client's goals. You also have an awareness of how much they understand about adolescent development.

I suggest you begin the second coaching session by placing in front of them a summary of their stated goals from the last session. This should be a significant list. Make sure it is organized by sections in order to help them quickly understand it. For example, have one section entitled "Goals for the family's health" and another section entitled "Goals for improving my relationships." Allow them time to review this list. Be silent as they look it over. When they are done reviewing the list, ask them the following questions: How do you feel when you look at this list? Coach - be prepared to offer encouragement, as they may feel overwhelmed by the volume of goals. Remind them that you will help them focus on 3-4 key goals and that progress in one area often results in progress in others.

> What, if any, surprises are in your list?
> What changes/additions/deletions do you want to make?

Ask them to select 3-4 key goals they want to begin to work on. Coach - write out each goal they specify. Under each goal, ask them the following questions and record their answers.

> What personal barriers do you anticipate?
> What other barriers might you face?
> How will you overcome these possible barriers?
> What resources do you personally have to help?
> What other resources do you want to utilize?
> What action steps will you take? Coach - list them in order with date of completion.
> How will things be after you have completed your action steps? Describe fully, utilizing your senses of seeing, hearing, feeling and possibly smelling and tasting.

THIRD AND SUBSEQUENT COACHING SESSIONS

My remaining sessions typically incorporate the following format:

> Tell me about how things have been since we last met.
> What resources did you utilize to accomplish that? OR

What obstacles kept you from achieving that?
How will you continue to work on that goal?
What will you do to move forward?
What do you want to focus on today?
What action steps will you take?
When will each step be completed?
Describe the result of completing those actions. Include your sense of hearing, seeing, feeling, and even tasting and smelling if appropriate.
How will you celebrate completing those action steps before our next meeting?
What could hold you back? How will you overcome that?
What personal resources will you utilize?
What other resources do you want?
Where and how will you get them?

Coach - make a record of the action steps they are committing to. Send those written steps to them shortly after this session with an encouraging note.

As mentioned earlier, your parent clients will benefit from understanding adolescent development along with parenting style development. Education may be a part of the work with them. I handle the education component in two ways. Sometimes I utilize the moment to introduce information. If my client George tells me that his daughter Jenny has been questioning rules she had never questioned before, I ask about his awareness of adolescent development. If it is new territory, I ask his permission to pause the coaching, provide some information, and then go back to coaching. During this time I provide information that will help him understand where that his daughter is coming from. For example, I provide a quick summary of the appropriate information above, and say something like, "This means it is a natural part of her development at this age to begin to question things. She is starting to think for herself about things like what is wrong and right." Then, as a coach again, I ask, "How can you utilize this change as a discussion starter? How will you ensure you listen to her and invite her to share her opinions? How do you want to renew your connection with her? How will you effectively shift from simply stating a rule to engaging with her to define the new rules?"

Other times, I follow a session with an email that includes both encouragement and also some pertinent information for them - oftentimes in the form of an article or website link. I encourage them to read it before our next session by letting them know that during the next session I will ask them for feedback on their reading. The feedback is usually quite positive and includes some "ah-ha!" moments they experienced.

> *"Other times, I follow a session with an email that includes both encouragement and also some pertinent information for them - oftentimes in the form of an article or website link."*

As an example, let's consider our client 'Susan'. She worries that her daughter, Alicia, may be depressed. Alicia has become quieter, spends more and more time in her room, has withdrawn from her friends, and seems to have little to no energy. I provide Susan with articles about signs of depression in adolescents. I ask her thoughts on how to initiate a discussion with her daughter about these concerns. I ask Susan about her awareness of important community resources and provide links in a follow-up email.

CLOSING THOUGHTS

Coaching parents is very rewarding. Do your preparation and you will be ready to help parents develop better lives for themselves and their children. I have loved my work with parents and am often rewarded with seeing how the children grow up to become wonderful parents themselves!

Karen Wrolson, MS has an extensive professional history working with challenging teenagers. For over 20 years Karen assisted in the development and direction of two schools for at-risk teenagers. As the Director and Counselor of these schools, she worked with over 800 teens and their families. Both schools had exceptional results including a decrease in the student dropout rate, an increase in individual GPA's, an increase in individual school attendance, a decrease in school rule violations, as well as monthly involvement in community volunteer work.

In her company, Excite Ed! Karen offers customized staff development to businesses as well as educational presentations on multiple topics to area groups. She serves as a Certified Professional Coach to parents of children of all ages.

Karen has a Master's Degree in Counseling, a Master's Degree in Education, as well as being a Certified Professional Coach. Her 20-plus year professional background, combined with her extensive educational preparation, make her well served to help others improve the quality of their lives.

Karen (and her cat) moved from WI to CA in 2011. She gives back to her community by assisting schools with at-risk students.

www.excite-ed.com

BENEFITS OF COACHING ALL GENERATIONS
Robbie M. Johnson

Coaching is beneficial to each generation in specific, similar ways. Because it is personal, individual objectives are the focus of the coaching relationship.

> *"Because it is personal, individual objectives are the focus of the coaching relationship."*

GENERATIONAL AND DEVELOPMENTAL INSIGHTS

The word generation has a propensity to signify differences. The term broadly categorizes individuals by birth during a specific time frame. A close look at the description of the time frames highlights major Western societal events during the era that had some degree of influence for shaping certain behaviors, thoughts, and ideas by which the generation is generally identified. A search of generations may offer related events of these periods such as:

- Traditionalists (1939-1947) – World Wars I and II and the Great Depression
- Baby Boomers (1948-1963) – civil rights and the women's movement
- Generation X (1963-1978) – 80's recession and commercialism
- Generation Y (1979-1991) – rapid change of technology

The descriptions and differences are from events that are real and historic; the implication is one of a changing society's behavior and perspectives. It is important to acknowledge and be aware that people of earlier generations (1939-1978) will have an emotional and psychological attachment to their events that the later generations may not understand and / or connect to in a similar manner. The earlier generations endured actions and behaviors that changed the societal environment into what the younger generations now experience. For instance the diversity of schools, communities, and the workplace as experienced today were nonexistent for the Traditionalists and Baby Boomers. Likewise, the younger generations will develop a different emotional and psychological attachment to the events of their era. Earlier generations experienced life in both the before and after society that resulted from their events. Some may find it difficult to adjust to the changes such as the use of technology and world views. Centered on their experiences, some behaviors and perspectives may be perceived as challenges to values and value systems. All generations can learn from each other.

> *"All generations can learn from each other."*

There is homogeneousness among all generations which is humanity. That is to say all generations are people. It is the humanity perspective of generations that will be used in examining the benefits of coaching. Research and studies of various disciplines have documented the lifespan development of humans. Various theorists and theories have established guidelines of expected development and growth associated with each stage in a life span. The stages are the same for all generations and are identified as conception to birth, infancy, toddler, pre-school, schoolers, adolescence, young adulthood, middle adulthood and late adulthood.

Before an individual has any consciousness of an external societal environment that may influence development, the individual is being developed; growth and transitions occurs through life span stages. The broad developmental process includes physical, cognitive, social, and personality during each stage. Sectors of the developmental process incorporate a complexity of contributing entities from family, church or religious affiliation, school, community, and friends, (the people factor) plus contributing factors from culture, communication, experiences, resources, media, etc. Results of the developmental process vary because all of the contributing entities and factors can be dissimilar in their own existence. A brief explanation: the family unit exists and is dissimilar in existence because it is multifaceted and what constitutes the structure of family is varied in perspective. Communities exist and vary by head of household, education, income levels, and housing. Schools exist and vary by public, private, charter, home school, low income, magnet, staffing, and curriculum. Church and religious affiliations exist and vary by beliefs, practices, traditions, rituals, and faith.

Individuals are not given a choice of placement in the environment that will influence his or her development; the variations in environment result in very unique individuals. These unique individuals share characteristics and basic requirements in each growth stage that are essential in overall development, such as wanting to belong, the need to feel safe, being valued, and a stable environment. People are relational beings; the desire to belong, to be affirmed and respected, is intergenerational. Awareness of generational differences and the similarities of humanity provide an opportunity for coaching that is beneficial to all generations based on what coaching is, which is discussed later.

Acknowledgement of the growth stages and process enhances awareness of individual uniqueness. Every person has a unique story that will bring variances to the coaching partnership according to his or her developmental experience. Understanding one's own process is imperative and can be considered a transition from self-concept to self-awareness.

Self-concept is how you see yourself through your developmental lens shaped by contributing entities (people factor). The question is what deposits have your contributing factors (culture, communication, experiences, and resources) and contributing entities (family, religious affiliations, community, and friends) made into your pool of beliefs and value system that defines who you are?

Self-awareness requires an inquiry and modification of self-concept based on exposure and learning new information while transitioning through life stages. It is an investigative process. As transition occurs, examination of childhood beliefs during a later stage can present tension as well as opportunities. A person may encounter a variety of understandings through this investigative process because positive and negative behavior and ideology has been taught and learned. Continuous modifications in the process of knowing who you are generate the transition to self-awareness. The more you know about your authentic self the greater your self-awareness. This transition influences how a coach performs in the coaching relationship; the authentic self of both the coach and the client will prevail in appearing during the coaching relationship. The ultimate question for the coach is, "who am I bringing to this relationship?" The coach also asks, "who is coming to partner in this relationship?" The coach then ensures that their "who" keeps the space open for the "who" of the client.

> *"Self-awareness...is an investigative process."*

Roles include those of sibling, child, employee, supervisor, parent, teacher, friend, etc. Development and growth are taking place before consciousness of roles.

A positive and supportive demeanor along with encouragement signifies forward movement, recognition of effort and achievement, and the coach is walking with the client as a partner. As a coach, consider your own demeanor and focus. What are your strengths, values, beliefs, biases, insecurities, and what is your passion? How do you ensure that coaching is truly about the client and their strengths, values, beliefs, biases, insecurities, and passions?

A Different Role: Coach

Coaching provides a unique opportunity for self-exploration of the area that an individual designates for change. The individual can be from any generation as discussed at the beginning of this chapter. The coach creates a positive and supportive collaboration. Coaching is helping people reach their potential through a partnership by asking probing, clarifying, and thought-provoking questions. The partnership is jointly cooperative relationship to clarify the present circumstances, identify where the individual wants to go in the future, and strategizing ways to get there. This coaching relationship is very different from the hierarchical and authoritative structures that are prevalent in life and most relationships experienced throughout developmental stages (structures that are common and experienced in families, schools, organizations, communities, workplace, and government).

Typical roles involve telling, suggesting, recommending, seeking control, talk a lot, plus at times even assume, order, blame, demean, and demand. Some of the behavior is appropriate in context, some is not appropriate, and all are inappropriate in coaching.

Life is full of noise and distractions, people are attached to cell phones, some type of screen, and headsets which are near the top of the list of distractions. You can count on at least one phone ringing in a meeting, seminar, class, program, wedding, or funeral. Cell phone conversations fill wait time in lines, doctor's office, library, restaurants, salons, and grocery stores. We hear the noise because of the ability to recognize by ear, one of our senses without paying attention to interpret what is heard.

Coaching allows an individual to step outside of the fast pace and busyness that seems to have engulfed living to explore and learn. Learning is achieved as a result of exploration and investigation, reflection, and journaling to list a few of the methodologies. Coaching quiets the noise and establishes a safe place for being heard because the coach is really listening. Listening is giving complete attention to gain understanding. It is an intentional action. A coach listens with total focus and demonstrates engagement in the conversation with brief acknowledgements such as, "wow," "tell me more," "that's great," and "what else?" Listening is an essential skill for effective communication and is beneficial for all generations and socioeconomic levels. Listening provides value because being heard and understood opens doors to awareness and planning; this provides usefulness personally or professionally.

> *"Listening provides value because being heard and understood opens doors to awareness and planning..."*

In the coaching relationship, asking lots of probing and thought provoking questions provides an opportunity for a client to think and express what is important to him or her and really focus. Probing questions, also open-ended, opens the door to exploration. A note: "why" questions are avoided because it is perceived as an attack so the answers become an excuse, a justification, or blame. Close-ended questions, resulting in yes or no answers, keep the door closed by limiting exploration. Asking open-ended questions offers a shift from telling, which is experienced in authoritative and/or hierarchical structures previously discussed. Asking is a tool that is beneficial because of the potential to equip and empower by encouraging critical thinking and allowing the clients to discover things about themselves. Equipping and empowering is about the client, and is beneficial for all generations.

The coaching partnership must have commitment from both parties to establish cooperation and trust for the desired results. The commitment of the coach is to keep confidentiality, to operate in a professional and ethical manner, to encourage and hold the client accountable. The client's commitment is to do the things he or she verbalizes, to explore, and to be held accountable. The co-created agenda fosters a future-focused relationship between the coach and client.

COMMUNICATION

Communication is intergenerational and essential in the coaching relationship. Communication, in general, consists of language that are words, signs, and symbols, and speech which is vocal communication of the language. Communication is both verbal and nonverbal (known as body language). Communication is two-way and involves a sender, a receiver, and a message. Words do not have universal meaning. A dictionary offers several meanings of a word, and meanings can also be defined by culture, subcultures, groups, and professional organizations or industries (known as jargon).

Communication occurs when the sender (originator) transmits a message, and there is a receiver. The message travels through a noise zone that may interfere with the interpretation of the message. The noise zone contains distractions from word meanings, usage, jargon, and culture which may cause misunderstanding and misinterpretation. A receiver is going to filter and interpret the message through their lens of understanding. The receiver may not be listening attentively. An example is a game called Pass the Message. A person starts a message by speaking or whispering it to someone (other players are unable to hear what was being said). Whatever was said is then repeated from one to the next to each player until it was told to the last player, who then says it out loud for everyone to hear. The message said out loud at the end is different from what the originator said, and many times the originator does not recognize any of what the last person said out loud. The message was altered by each player.

A coach, who understands the elements of communication, is positioned to effectively interact with individuals from any generation. For the coach it is an essential part of their role to ask for clarity and to paraphrase what was said to ensure understanding of what is spoken. The coach is aware so they listen to the words and figures of speech that the client uses, and use the same language in conversation to connect. Body language speaks nonverbally; it is unspoken thoughts expressed by facial expressions, gestures, movements, and shifts of the entire body. Messages can be positive, negative, or neutral formed through biases, approval or disapproval, satisfaction or dissatisfaction, etc. Body language may sometimes supersede verbal speech. Now for a self-awareness pause for the coach - how is your body language?

> *"Now for a self-awareness pause for the coach –*
> *how is your body language?"*

For this chapter, three persons from different generations were interviewed regarding the coaching experience. The Baby Boomer is female, married, a skilled technician, college graduate, and homeowner. Generation X is female, married, professional, college graduate, and homeowner. Generation Y is male, single, military, with some college. Annual income levels range from less than $25,000 to $45,000. Results of coaching interviews indicate similarities among the three and the differences speak to individual areas of interest.

When asked what the overall benefits of the coaching experience were, the similar responses from each included: increased self-awareness, a more positive outlook, generating positive energy, forward thinking, and forward movement. Self-awareness was the top benefit for each; it was viewed as a game changer for living a better life. Each person indicated having more confidence and belief in self. Goal setting and achievement were responses from Baby Boomer and Generation Y. Additional benefits for the Baby Boomer included replacing low self-esteem with confidence and having someone to listen. For Generation X it was the ability to gaze into the mirror of self with a sense of confidence. "Coaching helped me see how my life was determined by my decisions (or indecisions). I have a choice and I have the right to exercise my choice. I cannot leave it up to someone else to choose what path or direction to follow. It helped me stop being scared to make a decision and choose a side." Generation Y liked being held accountable which made him want to do more. He liked the accomplishments made through the process of having to report back to someone.

As stated previously, coaching provides an opening to exploration; each person had areas of specificity. The areas are related to life status, ultimate career goal and shifting.

GENERATIONAL COACHING STORIES

The Baby Boomer is very entrenched in her religious beliefs and her relationship with God. She is committed to her study time and seeking guidance for anything that she does. She prays for her family, friends, and customers. Her beliefs are the core of who she is as a person. She feels God has given her a passion for female ministry. After coaching, she learned that she does have time in her life to achieve her goals. "My self-esteem was low." She said she felt what she sought was inside of her and she did not know how to get it out. Age was a barrier for some of her goals because she thought it was too late. She went to school and made the Dean's List the first year. She developed organizational skills and strategic thinking to achieve a goal related to her passion, which was to help women achieve their potential. She organized and held a conference for women and started a small group. She learned to listen with intentionality and purpose to encourage others because of her growth in confidence. She is using what she learned to seek better opportunities in her career and other projects of interest. "I love the changes in me. The most relevant transformation was self-awareness." The shift did include times of tension; as coaching supported then encouraged shifting the transformation of self-confidence started to take place, "there was no support from my family even though the changes were noticed. I became an overcomer." She took charge of who she is instead of allowing the family's behavior to stop her progress. "Coaching sessions helped me to step outside of my busyness to prepare and prioritize daily. I take time to specifically write what I desire to accomplish weekly, to encourage myself and speak positive affirmations to me." She stated growth occurred in accountability and responsibility. She uses skills to affirm and support women who she meets through her profession; she said "people just need someone to listen, and I thank God for allowing me to be that person."

> *"Coaching sessions helped me to step outside of my busyness to prepare and prioritize daily."*

Generation X completed college, is progressing on the job, and is active in her church. She learned how to see herself in relation to all her experiences, people, situations, and other relationships. "I have the ability to gaze unafraid into the mirror of me." She states, "Everything has a purpose in how it is used to build upon the person that you are. I learned that the tough questions are the ones you have to answer about yourself. It's the self-knowledge that will help you navigate through all the areas of your life. I learned I can stand by my choices and not necessarily have to explain or justify myself to anyone. This means making my value system real and actionable." She further described her experience:

> "What I have learned enables me to speak my mind; being comfortable with saying what I want and overcame fear. I choose my battles. It was difficult in letting go of old habits and ways of thinking. Change is hard, especially when it is buffeted by fear. It was hard to accept that I could be different and still be ok. It was hard to think I might lose friends or relationships that meant something to me, even if they were not good for me. It was hard to accept that I deserved more than what I was used to. I am a work in progress, and can find myself slipping at times. But it has been about self-awareness and recognizing what triggers me to feel a certain way, and knowing what I can do to be better. Transformation occurred with a positive outlook and in relationships with my husband, kids, family, friends, associates, and church members. I feel good about the changes I have made. I believe I gained respect by sticking up for myself. I believe I gained trust because I know that everything doesn't have to be about me. I allow people around me to flourish and be who they are, and I like being the listener - something I learned from

my coach! Coaching invaded the busyness of life by allowing me to step outside of all the responsibility for everyone and everything and focus on me. My coaching session gave me opportunities to slow down and literally stop and breathe. I based my importance on how much I was doing and the fullness of my planner. Coaching altered that mindset in three ways; it helped me to focus on defining my values, it helped in determining how people and things fit those values, and it helped me to see no is a good answer. It all boiled down to choices and making the ones that are going to fit and not frustrate, help and not hinder my plans for what is best for me. Coaching helped me to prioritize, make decisions, and say no to a request for unplanned activity. Thanks to coaching, I know I don't have to be busy to be important. Especially not busy as part of someone else's agenda and schedule."

Generation Y is early in the young adult stage, has completed a year of college, is single, and he is not sure of the next. He said he learned to put self in check often, which was not a practice prior to coaching. Transitioning to being a young adult, coaching helped him to evaluate all relationships, deciding who he wants in his close surroundings. His new inner circle is multigenerational because he values the diversity. "I wished I had been coached in high school to make a smoother transition after graduation. I would highly recommend it for high schoolers." He states coaching was different because during the school years, parents and teachers are telling, giving directions, advising and directing; no one is asking and providing the type of conversations coaching offers. He said the listening process was great because it ignited thinking and reflection that had not occurred for forward moving into the young adulthood stage and beyond. He developed a higher level of determination because of having to be accountable for specific tasks related to specific goals. Exploration of self-encountered tension occurred: "breaking old habits, procrastination, and being lazy, the challenge was necessary to move forward, these were barriers in achieving what I want." He learned to set short term goals regarding financial management by attending a seminar. Setting long term goals involved identifying decisions that will impact career and where he wants to be when retirement comes with specific timeframes and how he is working towards them. "I will keep an accountability partner to keep me on track because it's easy to get off." He described his coaching sessions as "stops in my busyness." He was constantly and consistently going and doing. "I was busy doing so much and nothing at the same time. I was doing a lot and accomplishing nothing. I learned to prioritize and focus. Most of my busyness included wanting to please everyone; coaching helped me to change my thinking. It was good to have someone listen and encourage, it feels good moving forward. I evaluate how to function and what to say yes to." He notes taking time to process decisions - what worked, what did not, and what has been beneficial. Since working all day requires doing what others want done, self-time gives peace of mind. His coaching experience will help him to evaluate his plan to achieve his ultimate goal of becoming an executive.

> *"...self-time gives peace of mind."*

These coaching experiences are centered in the humanity perspective. No one mentioned any societal environment events. The transition from self-concept to self-awareness is an added feature of their journey, and they feel good about the changes they have made. Each person highlighted specifics of coaching that made the experience unique to their day-to-day living. Having someone to listen made a difference for each. Observations indicate each person was equipped with new tools to use in multiple areas of their life and empowered to live differently than before coaching.

IN SUMMARY

It will be beneficial for a coach to understand some aspects of generational knowledge in a broad sense, while understanding every person as a unique individual. More important is that within the uniqueness are similarities in basic needs and desires embedded in the growth stages of life.

The coaching role requires shifting out of other roles because as parents, supervisors, co-workers, friends, siblings, counselors, therapists, teachers, pastors, mentors, and so many more, we are telling, advising, instructing, directing, and multitasking. We are in the natural flow of what we do which is not coaching. As the coach you get to create a future-focused relationship with your client, assisting them in reaching their potential.

Robbie Johnson, a native of Charlotte, NC, is the mother of two grown children and has three grandchildren. She is a licensed minister of The Park Ministries. Her educational background includes a Bachelor of Arts in Business Administration from Belmont Abbey College, a Master of Ministry Leadership from Rockbridge Seminary, and an earned Doctor of Philosophy from Oxford Graduate School. She received the President's Award for her dissertation entitled *The Relationship of Communication Training and Interviewing Skills for Teens*. She has fifteen years of Human Resource experience, eleven years of Accounting, and is an adjunct professor at Oxford Graduate School. Robbie obtained a Certified Professional Coach designation through the Center for Coaching Certification.

Robbie believes in authentic relationships, beginning with an intimate relationship with God that flows into our horizontal relationships. Her passion for learning affirms her belief that education and the process of learning are the keys to opening doors and opportunities. This passion led to Robbie founding Sowing S.E.E.D.S. Institute, Inc., a non-profit organization for youth job readiness training. She believes in developing self-awareness for understanding what you bring to the table of all relationships.

www.TransformationalCoachingLLC.com

CAREER AND TRANSITION COACHING
Dina Simon

When you were in your twenties what did you want out of life? When you were in your forties what did you want out of life? Priorities change over time. Often we set out on a path for one reason or another and we find ourselves either at a fork in the road with decisions on which way to turn or we find that we have reached the top of the hill and we thought the view would be much more rewarding! This is when a career and transition coach can assist others through an inspiring journey to determine what the person really wants in a job or career.

Whether it is a specific job or company a client is considering transitioning away from, taking stock in personal strengths is a great start. Next explore how to take their strengths and their transferable skills to move to a new opportunity. This is a great way to provide coaching value to a client. There are some comprehensive and powerful process steps that can be used in such a situation.

The following process has three areas of coaching work to conduct with a client who finds themselves in transition or is contemplating one. The first step in the process is to really uncover what his/her past performance has looked like to identify opportunities for where he/she will shine in the future. The second step in the process is taking inventory in functional tasks that he/she will grade or rank in priority of what he/she does well. The third step in the process is to take a look into the future. What has this exploration process brought to the forefront and how do you coach your client to set action steps to uncover their desired future work? Often this work is still within his/her current company and realigned with strengths and passion. If the client is contemplating a transition or a new career, this process will help them identify how to take themselves to that market.

STEP ONE: PAST PERFORMANCE PREDICTS FUTURE PERFORMANCE

When someone decides to leave a position, they take themselves with them. Spending some time reflecting on what worked for him/her in the past and what didn't work is well worth exploration. Similar to a behavioral based interview, it is important to find out what were the situations that the client thrived in and what were the situations that he/she did not. Ask the following questions multiple times to get them to think on multiple projects/jobs etc.

> *"Spending some time reflecting on what worked for him/her in the past and what didn't work is well worth exploration."*

Past performance questions:
- Tell me about a time when you thrived in your career.

- What was going on?
- Who was around you?
- What are the reasons you feel you were thriving?
- What changed over time?
- Tell me about a time when you didn't feel you were thriving?
- What was the situation?
- Who were the people around you?
- What was going on within the company?
- What have been your favorite job duties?
- What are the reasons?
- What do you like to do the least?
- What are the reasons?
- Describe your experience working on a team.
- Describe your personal leadership style.
- What about your past experiences do you want to take with you and grow upon?
- What aspects of your past do you want to be different and how?

As you ask these questions and take notes on the information that is shared, much more will open up. The client might have forgotten about all the work they have done until they begin to really open up and talk about it. Often people are heads-down doing the work that they forget to reflect on how it feels to do the work. What went well and what didn't. Take all of this information and it will be used to expand upon in the next step.

Coaching tip: Coach clients on updating their LinkedIn page and their resume once a year. Encourage your client through coaching to continually make new connections on LinkedIn as well as endorse their connections and ask for endorsements of their own. Going through this process is a rich way to reflect on the scope of contribution and will empower them to continuously reflect on their performance. This process is like a personal performance review. What projects did he/she work on? What were the results?

> *"Going through this process is a rich way to reflect on the scope of contribution and will empower them to continuously reflect on their performance."*

STEP TWO: TAKING STOCK

What strengths and gifts does the client bring into the world? Create an action plan around what new possibilities make it possible for the client to live primarily in that space. The race for talent will only increase over the next several years. Those that know their value and what they bring to the market or to an organization will be set-up for success. Choices in full-time employment and/or contracting roles will open the playing field. Taking stock of his/her strengths and revisiting it from time-to-time will motivate your client to bring focus and passion to his/her role.

Below is a sample grid for this "Taking Stock" exercise. The grid shows three columns:

1) **Greatest Strengths** – you want to ask your client to reflect back on the conversations in step one and add additional areas in which he/she has the greatest strengths to bring to the table. Often times these are the tasks that many recognize the client as a leader or subject matter expert in. You want them to fill in 10+ areas of strength.

2) **Average Strengths** - you want to ask your client to continue with the exercise and list areas that they are good to average in. Things that they don't mind doing; they may not be called in to be an expert, they can hold their own. You want them to fill in 10+ areas of strength.

3) **Gap Strengths** – these are tasks and areas where your client does not have a great deal of skill or talent to bring to the table. These are areas where your client prefers to bring someone else in to help with the task or area of responsibility. You want them to think of and fill in as many as possible.

This "Taking Stock" exercise will create a clear visual as to what this client is passionate about and the gifts he/she bring to a job and company.

Listed below is an example of a grid with a sample of what comments look like.

Taking Stock Grid

Greatest Strengths:	Average Strengths:	Gap Strengths:
I am incredible in the following areas – these are my unique strengths	I am average to good in these following areas – I am okay with spending time focused on these activities	I am not good in these areas and/or just do not have the capabilities to do these tasks
I am an incredible coach – I have been told so by my clients, it is my passion, and I love to do it all day long. It gives me energy.	I am good at social media marketing. I could get better and I enjoy working on it.	I am not good at accounting. I don't understand it nor do I want to. It is easier for me to have someone else step in.
I am a dynamic sales leader and have a proven track record to lead and inspire sales teams.	I am good at creating the presentation slides to help tell the story to a client or prospect.	I am not good if technology breaks down. I call someone else in to help me so I don't make it worse.

With the short example above, it is clear that this person has a coaching and leadership passion. This person can live in the space of sales and marketing. They will not do well moving into an accounting or technical job function.

Take some of the conversation in step 1 and help talk through past experiences that went well. Create the "I have incredible strengths in ____". Continue to work through the exercise with your client. Give the client time to self-reflect and continue to add comments. Ask them to think about, "What do others come to you for your expertise?" "What areas do you think people quickly go to someone else on the team for?" These types of questions will help them come up with the answers to fill in the boxes with ease.

> *"Create the "I have incredible strengths in ____ ""*

This is a powerful exercise. So often we find that we aren't working even 50% of the time in the place where we have incredible strengths that we bring to the table. Sometimes we forget that we are extremely strong in an area that we walked away from and it would provide a tremendous value to all around us if we were doing it again. It can be powerful and surprising at the same time.

Coaching Tip: Ask your client how often they want to revisit this exercise. Explore the benefits. Take a look at what has changed. It will continue to be a great exercise to understand their value, unique strengths, and capabilities that he/she brings to a company. They may find that they aren't spending a lot of time in areas of great strengths and satisfaction. If they know it is short term due to other goals or priorities down the line, ask about how it fits now and in the future. Ask about their timeline for changing. They may realize there is an area that they want to increase skills in and seek training in that area.

STEP THREE: EXPLORING THE FUTURE

Now what? The client has gone down the path of the past and reflected on strengths and areas of great success. They have reflected on times that didn't go so well and areas that he/she doesn't have capacity or passion to spend time in. Now it is time to explore the future possibilities and create what their ideal vision looks like.

If your client is currently working: If your client is working now and in a discovery process to see if he/she wants to transition to a new role within the company or explore what else is out in the job market, the following steps are be recommended.

- **Evaluate the current job duties with the "Taking Stock" grid**
    - What are the areas of the current role that have alignment?

- What are the areas of the current role that do not have alignment?
- What opportunities are there in the current role to delegate tasks that are not a strength and then spend more time in the areas of greatest strength?
- What are the advancement opportunities within the current situation that create greater satisfaction down the line?
- What other roles within the company is your client considering moving into in the near or distant future?

- **What is the company culture in the current situation?**
    - How open is the culture for transition into another role within the company?
    - How does your client feel about their relationship with the leadership in his/her company?
    - What are the possibilities for being able to sit down and talk through their findings and come up with a career path or plan?
    - Which individuals within the company will he/she call upon to mentor or coach them?
    - What are the politics and dynamics in the areas of leadership or authority?

- **What other options are there?**
    - What special training or re-certification will enhance something that was once a strength or an area of interest to develop?

o   What do they want to change or have different to be happier in the role he/she is in?

Coach the client to design action steps for creating their future. It is very possible that an opportunity will arise within his/her current company. If your client is a strong contributor to the organization and he/she wants to stay and continue to work there, explore the opportunities to make the current situation better. If those opportunities get exhausted and the result is looking to move to another company, he/she will know that they did a lot of due diligence in making the decision on how to move forward. Alternatively, be open if your client wants to look outside their company.

If your client wants to explore other companies for a new role: If your client is currently working and they want to explore new companies, the above steps will be a huge help. The work is largely a deep reflection of past experiences and skills he/she brings to the table. Ideally have conversations about what type of leadership and company that he/she has worked well in. Take the time to really reflect on those themes to help uncover the type of company culture he/she wants to move to now.

If your client is not currently working: If your client is not currently working, than the section above helps them to become aware of what they want in a job and how to position themselves. Additional exploration is helpful so ask:

- What are the reasons your client is in a transition?
- What were the circumstances in their past positions?
- How do they want to manage their time and confidence during the job search?

You take yourself with you when you leave a job or company, so it is important to understand the situations that led to the decision.

> *"You take yourself with you when you leave a job or company, so it is important to understand the situations that led to the decision."*

If your client is able to be in a full-transition search this will be easier to move forward in a full-time capacity and openness versus someone who is currently working and challenged to carve out appropriate time to conduct his/her search.

ACTION PLANS FOR FINDING A NEW ROLE

What does the ideal role look like? Whether your client is working or not, the following coaching recommendations apply. Ask your client to describe the ideal job responsibilities based on all the work that you have done to this point. What does the role look like? What is a typical day like? Who is around him/her? What does the company culture look like? What size is the company? What are their thoughts on moving?

Get them really dreaming about what the role will look like and the work environment.

Where are those jobs today? What companies does your client think has those roles for them today or in the future? Who do they know at these companies to network with? What networking groups are in the area that attract people from those companies? What recruiting firms is he/she interested in working with? Ask your client to create an action list of the ten things he/she can do to research where these jobs can be found.

Networking and relationship building: Most recruiters will tell you that 75% or greater of the candidates that they place are people that were referred to them because someone thought highly enough to refer them to a company or to a specific role. In any job market, the value of networking and building solid relationships is a key component to success. When someone is in transition by choice or by force, they can be fragile and unsure of making a move to another company that they don't know a lot about. Scheduling informational interviews with companies to meet and greet people that are currently working for the organization can be a great way to discover alignment. Coach your client to build a list of people that he/she knows that work for ideal companies or industries to start gathering information. Ask your client their action plans for continuing to move forward. With each interaction there will be one to several action steps and follow-up opportunities. If your client is uncomfortable networking or building relationships in this manner, coaching through this is critical.

Coaching Tips on Networking: Walking into a room full of strangers can be very overwhelming to people. Alternatively, some people enjoy networking and meeting new friends. Work with your client to understand when they have networked in their career in the past and reflect on the results. Listed below are some powerful tips on networking:

1) **Where to go to network?** Recently my brother in-law shared that he wanted to move to the San Francisco area to work for a very specific company. He wanted to know how to break into the network of the organization. I asked him how he planned to go where the people of that organization are hanging out. What tradeshows do they attend in their industry? What events do they engage in or sponsor? In the physical area of the business, where do people go to hangout? How do you make yourself visible in those areas? Coach your clients to do some research as to where the best venues are to find the people he/she wants to find.

2) **Who will be there?** Often you know who is going to attend events prior to arriving. Many events are scheduled via social communication tools with names and contacts of others that have registered to attend. Ask you client about their research upfront on who will

be there and who your client wants to be introduced to. Coach your client to choose a goal to shake hands with X amount of people on their list. If he/she is unable to get information ahead of time, coach your client to set a goal as to how many new connections he/she wants when they walk out of the event.

3) **Bring a friend.** Coach your client to go with someone. It is okay to have a cohort with you at a networking event. It isn't okay to be glued to each other so that networking doesn't take place. If it means that your client will attend an important networking event versus not attending, bring a friend. Ask them their plan for how much time they will be with their friend versus meeting new people.

4) **What's the 30 second commercial?** Your client will be well served to practice how to share what he/she is looking to do in a short 30 second commercial. For example, "My name is Dina, and I am looking for a new role in a sales leadership capacity. How can I support you? Please support me - I am looking to network with people that are looking to grow their sales force. Who do you know here today that you recommend I make sure I meet?" In a coaching session role play with your client so they know what they want to say and how they will ask for connections or referrals. Ask them their ideas about business cards or something to give new contacts. How will your client make it easy to pass

personal contact information along to those they meet? For example, a box of business cards is easy and affordable to obtain.

5) **Follow-up is king.** So often people forget to take the time to say "Thank You" or "It was nice to meet you." Ask your client about their plans for connecting or following up with everyone he/she met with at the event. Brainstorm options such as LinkedIn or scheduling having coffee with anyone that he/she thinks expressed an interest in helping with the process. One connection leads to another connection. Ask about their plans for personal thank you notes, emails, or messages on LinkedIn. If someone takes the time to make an introduction or a connection for your client, ask them how they will follow-up with the original person that made the connection. If there is feedback on how the connection went and the results, the person that did the original referral will be more apt to continue to refer your client to other people.

6) **Keep at it.** As a seasoned professional networker I often find that I don't want to go to things I sometimes know make sense for me to go to for my work. I sign myself up and over commit and complain to myself in the car on the way to the event. Every time I walk out of one of those situations I find myself one step closer to achieving a goal or that my network has completely

opened up because I was at the right place at the right time.

A new role is secured: Coach your client to really reflect on this process and journey. What did they learn along the way? What did they learn about themselves? How are they going to continue to reflect on their learning? How do they want to thank those along the way that helped them get on this journey? How will they celebrate in accomplishing the new role?

> *"Coach your client to really reflect on this process and journey. What did they learn along the way?"*

Coaching tip: Coaching someone to imagine an ideal role while empowering them to take action to find that new role or job is extremely rewarding. It is a challenging process in a good way for both you the coach and for your client. Your client will likely experience a tremendous number of mixed feelings and uncertainty, as someone's career is so important to them. Enjoy this amazing opportunity to make an impact on your client's life to coach them through this journey and support their enjoyment!

Dina B. Simon is a Certified Professional Coach with over 20 years of executive leadership and sales experience within the human capital arena.

She is recognized as a dynamic leader that rolls-up her sleeves to help those she is working with bring their best selves to the table. Dina is often called upon to facilitate team and group sessions to help people think differently and create unstoppable problem solving.

Dina started her career in Human Resources and then moved into the staffing industry. For her, once a recruiter, always a recruiter. She is highly networked throughout the country and has a great ability to help people that are in a career transition investigate maximizing what they have done in the past and what they want to do in the future.

She serves as the President of Simon Says Give®, a non-profit her young daughter brought to light. The mission of SSG is **Kids Celebrating Kids** through the joy of birthday celebrations. Dina also serves as the CEO of Simon Says Lead™, a benefit corporation that is directly linked to Simon Says Give. Simon Says Lead works with individuals and client companies on a national basis to build leadership capacity by delivering workshops and coaching opportunities to help develop unstoppable leadership.

CLAP FOR CHANGE
Laura Posada

It's easy, it's productive – it's even fun. Yet we seldom stop and do it. I'm talking about clapping!

'Hey, I clap all the time,' you're thinking. Of course you do. You clap for a toddler taking those first steps, or for your home team scoring a victory, or for a great performance at your favorite theater. In this case I'm talking about clapping for yourself. When was the last time you stopped to do that?

It's a worthwhile question. There's more to clapping than putting your hands together – you can actually boost success when you pause to give yourself a hand. Motivation surges when you applaud the positive steps you take on the way to becoming your best self. Confidence grows when you celebrate each and every victory along the road to reaching your goals. Energy soars when you take a bow for those accomplishments, big or small.

Clapping for each change you make facilitates ever more positive changes. Affirmation fosters growth and helps us move forward to a brighter future.

In fact, the physical act of clapping has been shown to have a powerful positive effect on the brain itself. An MRI study published in the medical journal *NeuroRehabilitation* in 2011, for example, shows that clapping our hands is an effective method for stimulation of the brain. That's just one of the recent research studies on the power of applause. Studies on positive feedback go back over a century, starting with the work of psychologist Edward Thorndike as early as 1911, and moving on to the work of famed psychologist B. F. Skinner in the late 1950s. Skinner's groundbreaking experiments on positive reinforcement show that praise and appreciation motivate people to repeat and strengthen behaviors that are good for them.

In the decades since, a host of studies have focused on many aspects of positive reinforcement including applause. For example, a 1982 University of Wisconsin study on adult learning found that participants who reviewed their strong points after a bowling game improved twice as much as those who reviewed only their mistakes. The researchers' conclusion: a focus on the positive helps us tap into the desire to succeed.

> *"The researchers' conclusion: a focus on the positive helps us tap into the desire to succeed."*

In 2002, psychologists Jennifer Henderlong and Mark Lepper analyzed over thirty years of studies on the effects of praise. Their results reveal that praise can be a powerful motivating force when it is sincere and specific - that is, when the praise is based on actual achievement.

So even beyond personal observation, research shows that applause is a reliable motivator, especially when it's applied to real achievements, big or small.

So yes, it really is okay to praise yourself. It's great to let friends and family celebrate your successes, too. After all, there's a cheering section is wonderful, clapping right along with you to motivate you to push ahead to your next goal.

Are you ready to clap for yourself and the positive changes you're making in your life? If so, I bet you'd like to know how to begin. So let's talk about the Clap for Change movement, what it can do for you, and how you can be a part of it.

What's In A Name?

I reflected a long time on the name for my coaching enterprise. I am a believer in positive feedback and I know from experience that applause is a powerful tool. I've seen it propel teams and individuals to incredible performances, to results they themselves thought impossible.

So in thinking about my coaching enterprise, I thought about how I've always believed in the power of clapping – that wonderfully visible and audible way of showing support. I hadn't yet found a concrete way to incorporate applause into my new coaching enterprise.

During that time, I was interviewed by a journalist and long-time friend, Carlos. After we finished the interview and were talking as old pals, I shared my belief in applause with Carlos and told him how I love clapping for people's successes, because of the way it empowers them. He was fired up by the idea.

It happened that Carlos, too, was about to embark on a new project. On my way home I started brainstorming ideas, jotting things down informally, more or less doodling, adding our initials and mixing them up. At one point, I realized that the combination of our initials spelled: CLAP! It was a fun and exciting moment, because this serendipitous combination was almost an exact reflection of what I had been telling Carlos: how strongly I believe in positive feedback, in applauding people for each step they take that brings them closer to changing their lives.

> *"...applauding people for each step they take that brings them closer to changing their lives."*

The next day, Carlos e-mailed me a photo of a bunch of his friends clapping with him. "Hey," he said, "we're part of your movement!" The picture was so positive and full of energy, that when I saw it, the name for my coaching enterprise came to me instantly: Clap for Change.

It's a short, catchy name, and as you can see there is a great deal of substance behind it.
Clapping is a powerful motivator, a mantra, and now, it's a movement.

You're already part of it in many ways. Just think about all the times you clap. You clap to express approval, appreciation, or acclamation. You clap over and over at sporting events, concerts, parades, graduations. You clap to say "awesome job!" You clap to draw attention to something terrific! You clap for happiness at someone's success! You clap to celebrate!
Now, you can Clap for Change. In your own life.

Now it's time to learn to clap for yourself, to celebrate all your positive changes. Clapping for your own successes is expressive, exuberant, and effective in helping you achieve a life of growth, balance, happiness, and transformation. Clapping for change is a positive, high-spirited movement, and you can step in at any point.

A LITTLE SOMETHING EXTRA

As my friends, family, and clients can attest: I like simple.

Layers and nuances can tie us in knots or lead us off our course. Simplicity, on the other hand, encourages focus and focus is the most direct route to results.

I have learned that some layers are worth uncovering. Sometimes they add a certain zest, and I do like that, because zest is energy, and energy is a good thing. Sometimes layers also add depth, taking us a little further into the heart of the matter. We can all benefit from that.

Sometimes layers of meaning can enrich us, and even make us smile. That's especially true when the same phrases have different, and equally significant, meanings. Here's an example I love: You know how an emcee will say to the audience, after a great performance, "Let's give that band a hand!" We clap our hands like crazy because of course applauding is what "giving a hand" means. We're happy to do it. Then there's that other layer of meaning: when a neighbor gets stuck in the snow, or needs a ride to a doctor's appointment, we'll say, "Hey, let me give you a hand." Then we do. We don't applaud; instead we reach out a helping hand, literally or figuratively, and lend some support.

Either way you look at it, when we "give a hand," it's a terrific thing. The layers in this expression are completely positive, giving something good to both sides, the person giving a hand and the person accepting it.

So I often ask my clients: are you ready yet? Are you ready to give yourself a hand? That is, are you ready to applaud yourself and to help yourself out? To know they're both good things to do?

> *"Are you ready to give yourself a hand?"*

Let's take a look at how I coach my clients to get there.

MY PROFESSIONAL MISSION

My mission as a Certified Master Coach is to help every single client become his or her best self. Throughout the process, I'm by my client's side, to facilitate growth and transformation. In fact, it's my responsibility to help clients discover their unique purpose in this life. Not mine, not their mother's, not their significant other's. No, our work together is to find that individual's special vision for his or her own future.

There is great excitement in uncovering personal goals. Clients often arrive for their first session knowing they're seeking some kind of change, while unclear about what changes they actually want. Most people gain momentum with each session, and are soon inspired to think outside the box and to explore the fullest range of possibilities. My job is to create a safe, positive place unique to each person, a haven that fosters confidence and growth. There are few things as exhilarating as bouncing ideas off someone who wants you to succeed -- and that's a short definition of a life coach!

My responsibilities include helping clients with these key tasks: looking within themselves to discover their personal goals and vision; creating a detailed plan for achieving those goals; staying motivated and on track; and celebrating each success. At every point, I work with clients to access the tools available so they can draw on their innate power to move ever closer to the future they envision, with greater and greater confidence.

Yes, that *is* a lot. Then, it's a person's life we're talking about, and it takes a lot of thought, motivation, and energy for any of us to move forward to a happier, more balanced, and deeply meaningful place.

The great thing to remember is that all this is possible. Personal goals are within reach, simply by making one change at a time. With each positive change, we pause to clap! Then we move forward again.

> *"Personal goals are within reach,*
> *simply by making one change at a time."*

It's a process that works, at every age.

WHAT MY OWN COACHES TAUGHT ME

In my own life, I've been fortunate in having coaches who instilled in me a positive approach to success. They taught by example, with words, and with high expectations. Plus, they gave support and direction when I fell short, and praise when I made the mark.

As a young athlete growing up in Puerto Rico, I looked to my volleyball and softball coaches for inspiration. They encouraged me to do my personal best as a player, to achieve award-winning proficiency, and to be a team player.

My high school volleyball coach pushed us to the max, and at the same time, she showed us how to learn from mistakes and build on successes. She herself was a confident, high-achieving adult, someone to emulate both on and off the court.

When I was even younger, around ten or eleven years old, another coach took our entire team on a field trip to meet a famous boxer, a celebrity in my country. I'll never forget the boxer's speech. That's when I first learned of the Four D's: dedication, determination, discipline, and drive. With these four components, he told us, you can succeed.

I like sharing this wisdom because it affirms that it's within your power to achieve your personal goals.

Hoo-ray! The New York Yankees!

I've also had the privilege of seeing a legendary baseball team up close and personal. Since my husband Jorge played for the New York Yankees before he retired, I had a front row seat watching the team win five World Series championships. They were clearly doing something right! Of course they had tremendous talent in every position, and an intense work ethic; I've often thought that their closeness as a team was their greatest strength of all. It's hard for me to imagine a more cohesive group of individuals, consistently supportive of one another on both a professional and a personal level.

Their manager Mr. Joe Torre was an amazing leader, like an ideal father, knowing when to push and when to praise. There were affirmations all around the clubhouse, inspirational sayings to keep the team members focused on enhancing their prowess, their performance, and their personal and team goals.

> *"There were affirmations all around the clubhouse, inspirational sayings to keep the team members focused on enhancing their prowess, their performance, and their personal and team goals."*

It was an honor to witness the inner workings of one of the greatest teams of our time. As I watched the great become even greater, I came to understand that we all have it within us to become our greatest selves. Each of us deserves to find our highest purpose in life, to learn to focus on how to get there, and to ultimately celebrate the positive changes that we bring about.

These role models have inspired my key professional goals: to bring out the best in each of my clients, and to help them achieve the goals that give their lives balance, meaning, and joy.

FORMAL SCHOOLING AND REAL-LIFE LESSONS

We all have life experiences, planned and unplanned, that teach us vital lessons; sometimes more than we signed on for!

I'm an advocate of formal schooling because it means being prepared with the best professional training you can manage to move forward towards your goals. Studying a subject and mastering it empowers us with knowledge that we can apply to do our best work. Then, our learning continues.

I also have deep respect for the proverbial school of hard knocks. Despite its painful nature, I'm grateful to be a graduate of this "school," because there's nothing like facing unexpected challenges and set-backs, and even heartbreak, to teach you who you are and what you can do. The natural world teaches us that even a flower can't grow without breaking first, out of its protective seed pod, and pushing upwards, towards the sun and the air.

Like many people, I've benefitted from both formal education and real-life lessons. What I can testify to, as a life coach and as another person in this 21st century world we share, is that attitude is everything. No matter how tough the situation, it's how you decide to look at it that counts. Yes, you do get to decide. After you allow yourself to cry or scream or otherwise express your pain, anger, and frustration over a curveball in your life, you get to decide how to move forward. You aren't denying the curveball; you can choose how to understand it. It's amazing how a shift in perspective can turn the worst disappointments, the most unfair circumstances, into a new awareness, sometimes even a life-changing epiphany.

Whatever your educational and professional attainments, life continues to throw out challenges. No matter how daunting your personal set-backs have been, be assured that you can reframe them and move forward towards a new vision.

I'm not saying it's easy; it is how transformation begins.

How My Legal Training and Compassion Work Together

I was an attorney in my twenties, and my legal background has helped to shape my work as a coach in important ways.

In law school, we were taught to be objective above all else, and to be practical. It's a detached, black and white approach; it trained me to look at the issue at hand, understand the circumstances, and figure out how to get the best results.

Focus is the key word here. My legal training taught me to hone in on the essentials. I now share this skill with my coaching clients: when I look at a person's situation, I can be very practical so we can get right to the important issues.

There's another side to coaching that's equally important, and that's empathy or compassion.

Compassion gets us even deeper into the issues, into the heart of the matter. I'm drawn to coaching in large part because I know how important it is to be able to put yourself in another individual's position and grasp it from the inside out.

In other words, a coach has to care. You have to want to make a difference.

> *"In other words, a coach has to care.*
> *You have to want to make a difference."*

My background helps me to bring together these important skills on behalf of my clients.

A Very Personal Challenge

I certainly would not have chosen the circumstances that developed my compassion and a fuller appreciation of life and health. I was a carefree newlywed, enjoying life in New York City with my husband Jorge, when our first child was born. Our son was diagnosed with craniosynostosis, a life-threatening skull deformation, at birth. My husband and I had never heard the word, then we were soon immersed in medical terminology, hospitals, and surgeries. Our baby had his first 12-hour surgery at nine months and eight more surgeries in as many years.

We're fortunate that Jorge Luis received good medical care and is now enjoying a healthy life like other boys his age. The early months and years of his diagnosis were dark ones for our family, since we knew nothing of the condition and were frightened for our child. Over time, Jorge and I grew to understand what our son faced and how we could best help him, a struggle we wrote about in our book, "The Beauty of Love." We even came to see that our mutual struggle helped us to grow as parents, as a couple, and as human beings. Our son was a blessing from the start, and always will be. We owe him our deepest understandings of what this life is about: love, family, helping others, staying positive - more than words can express.

After our son's second surgery, my husband and I started the Jorge Posada Foundation. We wanted to share our knowledge of craniosynostosis with other mothers and fathers, increase research and awareness in the medical community, aid families needing a boost with medical care, and simply reach out to other frightened parents with moral support.

ON-THE-JOB AND ON-SCREEN TRAINING AS A COACH

We created a Mentors Program for the Jorge Posada Foundation, and as a founder, I was also the first mentor. In that role, I talked to other families going through the same situation, giving them advice on what was ahead of them and what had worked for us. Before long, people started contacting me, both for advice on dealing with craniosynostosis and for guidance in other areas of their lives. I heard especially from women trying to juggle everything, being a mom, working outside the home, and having a happy marriage, all the roles women are expected to manage.

I sensed I could make a difference, and I began hosting a television show for Fox International Channel, "The Survival Guide with Laura Posada." Over two years, I visited 26 families. I spent time with them, helped them figure out what was going on, and helped them discover tools to work through their specific challenges and to improve their lives. Essentially, I was their life coach, talking to each family member and coaching the entire family to get to a happier place.

This experience made me realize that I had the ability to motivate and inspire others. Still, I felt there was more to learn, and I wanted to have as many tools and techniques at hand as I possibly could. So I earned my Certified Professional Coach and then my Certified Master Coach designations. It's been a natural progression for me, as if life kept sending me signals and opportunities until I embraced my role as a life coach.

REASONS I COACH AND HOW I COACH

My overriding goal as a coach is to make a difference in each client's life by dedicating myself to his or her accomplishments.

My goals for supporting my clients encompass a wealth of positive changes: growth, transformation, balance, purpose, and joy. You already have the tools within yourself to bring about positive change, and a coach is there to help you access those tools. Working together, you can achieve the life of happiness and meaning that you envision.

> *"You already have the tools within yourself*
> *to bring about positive change,*
> *and a coach is there to help you access those tools."*

I've developed a simple four-step process that helps each person define his or her own goals and move towards them, with plenty of stops along the way to clap for positive changes!

An Overview of How My Coaching Works

Step One: Figure out what it is you want.

This sounds deceptively simple. I've found that even the most accomplished individuals, whether they're corporate executives, entrepreneurs, artists, or other high achievers, have yet to pinpoint exactly what is missing in their lives. That's not an obstacle; it's a beginning. All it takes is to know is that you're seeking something more and to have the courage to discover what that is.

My role is to help you uncover your personal vision for a brighter future.

There are many effective tools to help you find your way in Step One. For example, visualization can be a powerful technique, a way to guide you in discovering what it is you want for the future. When you're in a safe, nurturing environment, you can conjure vivid descriptions from deep within yourself of where you'd truly like to be. When you visualize this happier, more productive place, goals flow freely and transformation can begin.

> *"...visualization can be a powerful technique, a way to guide you in discovering what it is you want for the future."*

Step One is not a simple step; it is an exciting one because it brings you face to face with the best person you can be.

Step Two: Create a detailed action plan of what you're going to do, and how you're going to do it.

When I say detailed, I mean details, details, details. Then more details. As your coach, I'm not going to let you get away with simply saying, "I'd like to be healthier, so I'll start to exercise." No way. Instead, I'm going to push you with specific questions. I'm going to say, "Okay, good idea. How are you going to do that? Exactly what are you going to do to achieve your goal?" Let's say you answer: "Jogging." Then I'll pin you down even more! I'll ask you: "Where are you going to do it? And when? No, not just mornings – exactly what time of day are you going to schedule your run?" Then we'll make a list of what resources you want: a running program, running shoes, a running log, and so on. Then, more details. On it goes, until you have a very specific plan. With dates, times, every single detail. Because every detail is a step forward, and every step forward builds your confidence and gets you closer to the healthier, brighter future you envision.

Step Three: Start to execute your plan.

This is where we get down and dirty with those plan details, making them all happen. This is when you get up for that 6 a.m. jog or swim and enter it in your log.

Will you get discouraged? Well, let's just say you're not from planet Earth if you don't fall off course from time to time. We're human, not perfect. And remember: perfection is not your goal; your goal is to be a better human being.

It's an ongoing challenge to stay focused and to continue taking step after step. When you fade a bit, I'm here to help bring you back, with positive reinforcement and specific tools that you can then use independently.

For example, one of my clients is a young professional I'll call Ryan, to preserve his privacy. He came to me because he wanted to change his specialty at work. He was very specific about his goal, and we created a detailed plan that would bring him up to speed on the particular subject area he wanted to pursue. When the time came to approach his manager about making a change, Ryan found himself making excuses. "I'll mention it when I run into her in the hall," he told me, and then he laughed, because when he said it out loud, he himself could hear how evasive he was being.

So we brainstormed about how he could take a more direct, effective approach, and Ryan left with a specific time and date to request an office meeting with his manager. After he accomplished that important step, we clapped for his success.

Since Ryan wasn't completely satisfied with the outcome of his meeting, we created a step-by-step plan to investigate other job opportunities at other companies. He's in the process of that exploration now, and we clap for each step he takes along the way. Ryan is on track to make the positive changes he envisions.

My job as your life coach is to keep you on track

Step Four: Celebrate!

I believe it's vitally important to stop and applaud absolutely every achievement along the way to your goal.

Yes, my clients and I actually clap in our sessions whenever they make a change for the better, including small ones. I clap, and the client claps. This fun physical activity is a tangible reminder to praise ourselves when we succeed. Often between sessions, when a client reaches a goal, they'll text me: "clap clap clap." It's our code word for success. They tell me it makes them smile!

In a deep or visceral way, clapping for yourself helps your confidence grow, and helps you claim your pride in your successes. It reminds you that you're moving forward, step by step, to the life you envision. Clapping is a delightful expression of approval and positive reinforcement. It confirms that you're doing the right thing, and that you are moving towards your goals.

I urge you to give yourself a hand every time you have a success. In addition, I encourage you to celebrate each success with family and friends because their positive feedback will give you confidence, keep you motivated, and spur you on to achieve your next goal. That's the reason we clap for change.

In time you'll see that clapping for change is more than a bonus, more than the icing on the cake: it's essential to your progress.

Progressing to your goals is what it's all about, and what I want for you. That's because I know that moving into your unique vision for your future will make a difference in your life, and most likely, in the lives of those around you.

If you're ready to seek your dreams, you deserve applause. Whenever you start, I clap for you. As you keep moving forward towards your truest self, I clap for you. At every step.

I hope you're ready to join the Clap for Change movement. Most of all, I hope you continue to celebrate your successes and to clap for yourself all along the way to your best life. You deserve a standing O!

"You deserve a standing O!"

Laura Posada is a mom, attorney, certified master coach, certified personal trainer, TV personality, and philanthropic icon. She co-produced and hosted *Manual de Supervivencia con Laura Posada*. She appears on NBC's *Today Show* giving coaching tips. She co-hosted *Tu Vida Mas Simple* and appears on Univision's *Despierta America* as a lifestyle expert.

In *Fit Home Team*, 2009, Laura illustrates the triumph of raising a healthy and fit family. In 2010 Laura released her second book, *The Beauty of Love: A Memoir of Miracles, Hope, and Healing*, where she shares her family's deeply moving and uplifting story following the diagnosis of a life-threatening skull deformation ten days after the birth of their son, Jorge Luis Jr.

Awards
- 2006 Puerto Rican Family Foundation Excellence Award
- 2008 "Always Inspiring Woman" by Siempre Mujer
- 2009 Latino Trendsetters by Defining Trends Magazine
- 2009 Super-Mom by the Magazine Selecciones
- Inspiring Words from the Latin Pride National Awards
- 2011 Distinguished Women Award from El Diario
- 2012, 2014 News Lady of the week by CNN in Spanish
- 2014 Wall Street Journal Donor of the Week
- 2014 Woman of Impact by Univision Network

www.LauraPosada.com

THREE SECRETS TO SELECTING A COACH
Bill Shell

Over the course of my career working with small business owners and executives I've had the opportunity to engage and assess a variety of coaching and consulting relationships. Many have worked extremely well. Others were quite challenging. It is for this reason that I hope to share a few insights I've learned in the search, selection, and engagement of a coach for you or your business.

In this chapter, I will share three specific points for your consideration in maximizing effectiveness with your coach:

1) Identify your destination - learn the reasons you are starting the search for a coach and define your desired outcome so you are on the right path.
2) Identify your objectives (expectations and priorities) - before the search, identify your personal and professional requirements when working with a coach.
3) Identify your metrics - before you start the engagement determine how you will measure the effectiveness of the relationship, progress, and ultimate success of your coaching engagement.

Before we get started, here is a little background. My first coach and consulting mentor was Vince. He was a seasoned

IBM executive who really understood executives, owners, and the businesses they operated. He and I worked on multiple projects while I was with AT&T specifically targeting account teams and senior executives to brush up their selling and account management skills.

One day over lunch I shared with Vince my desire to eventually become a coach or business consultant. He smiled and over the next hour shared with me his life's journey and what he did to put himself in a position (then in his early 50s) to fully realize his dream of helping people help themselves through challenging business and life situations. He considered himself less of a coach or a consultant and more of a strategic advisor in working with his clients. He understood that sometimes he would coach the client and other times he would be more hands-on with recommendations and direction as a consultant. His explanation was my first real introduction to the difference in approach, process, and outcome for each client served.

It was during that lunch that he and I began a process of discovery. We spent time on the three questions I outlined previously. He asked me: "Bill, what do you want out of this opportunity of becoming a coach or consultant?" If I can help you get there what exactly do you want? Where do you want to go? When do you want to be there, and how will you know when you've arrived?" I re-interpreted these questions later in my career to mean, "Bill, what do you want to be when you grow up?" Knowing the path to my destination and understanding how I would know if I arrived. So simple and so profound. So with that in mind, let's start our time of discovery.

> *"Knowing the path to my destination and understanding how I would know if I arrived."*

LESSON #1 – IDENTIFY YOUR DESTINATION

First, what are the reasons you want a coach in your life or business? How did you come to that realization? More importantly, are you ready to own the experience, to be fully engaged and ready to act on the results of the coaching experience? Coaching success is not a spectator sport. It requires two people, equally and actively engaged, working toward a set of specific goals.

Observation: Experience has taught me that it is the client who desires something to happen and therefore leads the coaching relationship. If you are having a coach pressed upon you, chances are you will have a difficult time working with a coach - any coach - and the engagement will fail unless you address this up front and decide to engage. If your boss suggests you get a coach, or you decide to independently engage a coach, reflect on your objectives before taking action.

The first step in embarking on a great coaching engagement is for you to dig deep and understand your personal and professional motivations. Seek out the reasons. Here are examples:
- Enhancing self-awareness
- Stretching personally and professionally
- To be held accountable
- To increase learning
- Opportunities for ongoing personal and professional development
- Committing the time to gain new life and career skills

Timing is everything. If you're not ready for a coach, then don't engage one (there will be a better time and place).

Starting the journey well can greatly enhance your success as you reach the planned destination.

If you're ready to get started, here are a few tips and hints when looking for a coach or consultant:

1) Work with an International Coaching Federation (ICF) member coach:
    - First of all anyone can call themselves a coach or consultant. At this time there is no single group or regulating body that drives consistency. I have personally found that the ICF certification process

and associated Code of Ethics provide for a great platform and uniformity of approach. When asked, I recommend you work with a member of the ICF.

2) Understand their coaching process:
    - Every coach has a process for discovery and client engagement. Don't walk into your coaching experience blindfolded. Inquire as to their approach and process before selecting your coach.

3) Discuss private vs. public information:
    - In simple terms, inquire about what is private information for them and what is not. Most coaching clients have a simple expectation for privacy – keep private the things we talk about during our coaching sessions. Some coaches have a very different approach and can potentially share more than they should with the coaching sponsor (your boss). This is a violation of the ICF Code of Ethics. Set the ground rules early.

4) Confirm their style and your style complement one another:
    - We're all different. Sometimes that's good. Sometimes it can cause real roadblocks to open, honest communication. Challenging your line of thinking and stretching yourself can be a good thing. Be intentional with how far you want to push the boundaries. Be prepared to walk away from a potential coach that just doesn't feel right to you.

> *"Challenging your line of thinking and stretching yourself can be a good thing."*

5) Look for experience that adds value to your personal / professional journey:
    - Few of us want to be coached by someone just like us. Look for a coach that adds substantial value to your personal and professional journey. Look for a coach that: brings experience and wisdom you seek, asks great questions, or who is one that you would be proud to call an associate well after the formal engagement is completed.

6) Understand their expectations from your engagement:
    - Yes, coaches have expectations from each client they serve. What are their expectations of you as a client? Ask them. If they can't share their expectations of the coaching engagement, don't hire them.

7) Spend time with them before signing on:
    - No one ever said that your first meeting with the potential coach is the first meeting of your formal coaching engagement. Get to know the coach a bit before signing on the dotted line. Understand their priorities and their personal and professional journey. Make sure they are a great fit for where you want to be, not where you are right now.

Lesson #2 – Identify Your Objectives and Priorities

Most coaching candidates seek out expert guidance of professional coaches who are both successful coaches and also successful business professionals. They demonstrate a genuine interest in assisting you, the coaching client. Your professional coach has your wants and s in mind from the onset of the coaching engagement.

Here are a few of the potential areas for focus during considering your coaching engagement:
Your coach is available to:
- Help you look at the big picture for your life and career.
- Guide you through the process of enhancing your professional skills.
- Provide open and candid exploration of your strengths and weaknesses.
- Help you identify opportunities in your life and career.
- Connect you with potential resources that don't fit their area of expertise.
- Support you through the transitional periods in your career.
- Help you find balance in your personal and professional life.
- Actively listen to the challenges you face as you set and pursue goals.

- Work closely as you carry out stated career goals and plans.
- Hold you accountable and focused on the goals you established early in the coaching relationship.
- Expand, explore, and encourage you as you discover the potential in your life and career.

How will you know your coaching engagement is meeting the outcomes you established?

Here are a few things to look for as confirmation that your expectations are being met:

- During the coaching process, you become more open to change and transition, exploring new possibilities, and learning from others.
- You become more in tune with your personal and professional goals, and learn a process for achieving them.
- You are inspired by the process and gain a great deal of satisfaction from it.
- You gain a better, deeper commitment to understanding and growing.
- You handle challenges and stress more effectively, confronting problems and working toward solutions to problems as they are identified.

- You feel comfortable with and challenged by your coach.
- You are able to open up and speak directly to your trusted and respected advisor.
- You are able to relate to the process your coach brings to the engagement and gain value and insights each step of the way.
- You look forward to continuing the coaching relationship and become an advocate of the experience for others.

The key to a successful coaching engagement is full engagement. Most of the complaints I hear surrounding a bad coaching experience deal with the lack of communication and identification of unmet expectations. What is left unsaid becomes more powerful than what is said.

> *"The key to a successful coaching engagement is full engagement."*

Another problem I encounter is unrealistic expectations by the person being coached – that would be YOU. Here are a few of the more fun expectations I have had clients express to me:

1) "I need to come out of this coaching experience a changed person - ready to climb new career heights and achieve my life and career dreams. You can help me do that, right?"

2) "When I complete my coaching I know I'll be ready for that promotion I need. Surely they can't turn me down after I go through all of this stuff."
3) "Can you share with me your secret sauce, the recipe that ensures success with each person you coach?"
4) "If I have to go through this process, then you better be really good because I can be a little stubborn at times."
5) "Since the boss tells me I need this, I guess they are right. How long will it take to get them to change their impression of me?"
6) "If you are my coach does that mean you guarantee results?"

Of course I was a bit taken back by these expectations. Each person was genuinely interested in a great outcome. They just didn't understand the process and how to articulate what they wanted from their coaching experience.

So here's my question: what do you really want? What are your objectives? Write them down, prioritize them, and understand how they impact your present and future self. It's amazing to me how many people continue to complain about unwritten and unrealized dreams.

Let's get started: Write goals and prioritize them. Okay, now that you have them written down and prioritized, here are a few questions to ask your prospective coach (yes, it is okay for you

to interview them in the process):
- Tell me about yourself - your background, hobbies, etc.
- How did you become a coach? How long have you been a coach? Are you a member of the ICF?
- Tell me about what you have learned coaching?
- Describe your coaching approach.
- Tell me about your coaching process.
- How does coaching work with you? Tell me about the typical coaching session - schedule, process, tools used?
- How often do you typically meet with coaching clients? How long is each session?
- Give me an example of a coaching development plan.
- Will you tell my boss what we talk about?
- What guides you? What directs you? What drives and motivates you?

Once you have the opportunity to interview the potential coach, you have a choice to make: engage or not engage. If you have the ability to decide between a few potential coaches, here are a few items to consider for the final selection:
1) Can you see yourself being coached by this person?
2) Will your personal styles work well together?
3) Do you get the sense that the coach is interested in your objectives before his or her own?
4) Are they a good listener?

5) Did they give you direct, authentic feedback during your initial meeting, or seemingly confirm what they think you wanted to hear?
6) Do they understand what you do now and where you want to go (life and career)?
7) Can you see yourself being held accountable for actions agreed upon?
8) Can you laugh with this person?
9) Can you have serious conversation with this person?
10) Can you trust them?

Chances are if you answered positively to at least seven of these questions, then you have found a good coaching candidate. If not, then keep looking.

LESSON #3 – IDENTIFY YOUR METRICS (HOW YOU WILL MEASURE SUCCESS)

There are a few tried and true beliefs I have in life and business.
- *First – before you start the process understand your endgame.*
- *Understand that great outcomes must be measurable.*

The same rings true when engaging a coach (or business consultant).

First of all, measuring success in coaching is not about pure return on investment (ROI). Anyone who enters into a coaching relationship with the expectation of X% ROI is simply misguided. Yes, most successful coaching engagements can see increases in personal confidence, better relationships, and enhanced overall performance.

Most successful coaching relationships (where measureable results are expected) start with well-defined goals and objectives. Write it down to start with so you can measure it. Sounds pretty simple and at the same time I'm amazed at how many clients seemingly are disappointed when unset expectations are, in turn, unmet. The key is to take the time to set down on paper your goals (the end in mind) and how you plan to measure them (your desired outcomes).

> *"The key is to take the time to set down on paper your goals (the end in mind) and how you plan to measure them (your desired outcomes)."*

Most successful coaching engagements leave the person being coached with increased confidence in their role, a better place within the organization, and life in general. Many times the coaching process empowers those being coached to work through the personal and professional demons and roadblocks that hold them back, thereby creating a platform for better, faster professional growth.

So how will you measure your next coaching engagement? Now is the time to determine what your next time looks like, even before you start the process of search, selection, and hiring of the coach that will take you to your next level.

In closing...I return to my story about my friend and mentor Vince. Vince is far from a fictional person made up just for the pages of this book. Vince was and is a very real person. I sat with him through many hours of coaching, consulting, and training as we helped experienced, seasoned sales and account teams confront their professional demons and roadblocks.

One of my strongest memories of Vince is his ability to listen. The first time in my career I experienced active listening skills (well before we started calling it that) was with Vince. Much of his success in sales and executive coaching over the years was due to his ability to listen for both what was being said and for what wasn't being said. He listened so intently that the person speaking thought there were only two people in the world at that very moment: them self and Vince. His approach to listening is the example I strive for to this very day.

Another coaching skill that Vince demonstrated was his ability to ask simple, open-ended questions that compelled the person being coached to actively engage in the conversation. To some, it appeared that Vince was lacking knowledge. It was quite the opposite. His power wasn't in the knowledge he possessed, it was in the knowledge he pursued. As a great coach, Vince learned that the people he worked with didn't really care about how much he knew, they cared about how much Vince cared about them and his desire to see them become all they could be. He was able to see it for them before they could see it for themselves, and believe they could reach new heights in life and career. By the end of the coaching process, they knew every great idea was theirs alone. The process he took them through to get there was amazing to watch.

> *"His power wasn't in the knowledge he possessed, it was in the knowledge he pursued."*

Vince is significant to my story and recommendations in this chapter. Simply put, he taught me so much that was important for me to know early in my coaching career, brought me to the doorstep, and left me there. It was at lunch one day I shared with Vince that I wanted to become a coach and consultant just like him. He seemed quite excited at the prospect and spent the next few minutes asking the reasons, the how and when related questions. He then outlined the many talents he believed I bring to the role and how I could achieve success. Of course, I was feeling quite smart, positive, and a bit full of myself. Here was this respected, experienced, successful, coach and business executive singing my praises…bring it on Vince, tell me more.

Then came the other shoe to drop…the one that brings me full circle to where we are today.

After all the compliments and visions of success Vince placed at my feet came the words I didn't want to hear. "Bill, are you sure you're ready? You'll be a great coach and consultant some day, are you sure now is the right time? What experience are you lacking? How can you impact those you serve as you grow, learn, and practice the craft? How will you figure out your own journey, write your own story? What do you think, Bill? Have you considered getting your first real coach?" What he was helping me arrive at was the realization that it wasn't good enough just to observe, learn, and do. I had to actively engage, to become a player in the game, not just watch the game. It was disappointing at the time, even a bit discouraging, and yet so true. If only I had been ready to act then; I wasn't. It took close to two decades for me to become confident in my ability to make Vince proud. During those years I was coached, I learned the process and craft. I experienced success and failure, all things we experience along the journey. I thought I'd never get over the hope and rejection of Vince's conversation over lunch that day; that was then, this is now.

So who is your Vince? What is your story? How did your story start? How will your story end?

The road can be long, hard, and at times totally overwhelming. Along the way you may want to give up, give in, and go on to whatever is next in your long line of career choices. For what it's worth, I highly recommend you stop and assess your next step. If it means you get a coach worthy of Vince's standards, then good luck in your search. Maybe it's your desire to become a coach like Vince. It's your choice. It's your life. It's your career. It's your decision.

Hopefully, I have shared a few words of wisdom along the way. If so, thanks for reading. If not, then chalk it up to a coach and consultant that just wanted to get published (that is supposed to be a joke). Seriously, I hope and pray that you find a great coach and mentor as I did in my, albeit, frustrating, and highly valued friend, Vince.

I dedicate my passion for coaching to the persons who have influenced me most. My father, my wife, and my best, most effective coaches.

My father is the wisest man I have ever known. Born a preacher's son, in the midst of the depression, he went on to get his doctorate in education. He was my first great teacher. He shared with me many things. Two have stuck with me throughout my time as a coach and consultant: patience and wisdom. I pray for them every day.

My wife early in her life was told by one of her first "coaches" (her high school guidance counselor), to never pursue her dream of becoming a nurse (apparently she just wasn't smart enough).

Today, she has a doctorate in nursing with an emphasis in leadership development (guess she was smart enough all long). She has been another example of how a gentle poke along the way can reap great results.

We all have a story, a journey. Where we've been and where we want to be. Where are you today? Where do you want to be in five years? It's time to decide.

As for me, I'm a coach.

> *"We all have a story, a journey.*
> *Where we've been and where we want to be.*
> *Where are you today?*
> *Where do you want to be in five years?*
> *It's time to decide."*

Bill Shell has spent his career directing and empowering fast growth, market driven companies in service, technology, retail, financial, and manufacturing industries. He believes that the owners and executive team first define the legacy of any business, and that they must personally own success and failure.

With extensive entrepreneurial and corporate experience, Bill is known as a driven, hands-on team leader. He has an extensive background in strategic planning and implementation, new business start-up and development, marketing, sales, franchising, distribution, operations, project management, budgeting and P&L, organizational development, and all facets of tactical business execution.

Since founding Legacy Market Services in 2004, Bill has led multiple business clients in their strategic and tactical planning and engaged with collaborative project teams in the development of new business ventures. He has served as an advisor to small business, and on corporate boards.

Bill@LegacyMarketServices.com

THE PHENOMENAL COACH
Evette Beckett-Tuggle

In my work to help others move beyond their self-imposed limitations to manifest the phenomenal greatness that is within each of us, I reflect on the magnificent gifts of inspiration and brilliance given to us through the spoken word by the late author, Maya Angelou. Ms. Angelou truly modeled the essence of phenomenal greatness in her poetry, books, and other genres of artistic expression, and by the way in which she rose above adversities in her own life to encourage others to do the same.

Her words helped us visualize a moment in time. Her manner of expression cast a mirror on our own experiences and increased our level of awareness. Her inflections made us feel something relevant, positive, and alive. In many respects, Maya Angelou is the embodiment of what I refer to as "The Phenomenal Coach." Her words affirm, inspire, and empower others to see, hear, and feel the possibility of moving ever upward toward a higher state of being.

PHENOMENAL WORDS

The spoken word is a powerful motivator. As coaches, what we say and how we say it are important in establishing rapport with our clients. One tool that coaches use in establishing client rapport is the use of "phenomenal words."

Phenomenal words are positive words that are used in the course of discussion with clients. They are words used in questions coaches ask and in affirmation statements coaches write and deliver to their clients. These words are phenomenal because they benefit clients in three ways:
- Phenomenal words <u>affirm</u> that what the client is imparting is relevant and of value.
- Phenomenal words <u>inspire</u> clients to express themselves.
- Phenomenal words <u>empower</u> clients to take action towards their goal.

Examples of phenomenal words include: *aware, balance, brilliant, calm, create, enlighten, imagine, opportunity,* and *visualize.* I will expand on this list further in the "Phenomenal Branding Chart."

ART AS INSPIRATION

Just as great writers and orators use images, illustrations, and quotes to stimulate our thoughts, discussion, and actions, so too do great coaches. Consider using any number of approaches at

> *"Just as great writers and orators use images, illustrations, and quotes to stimulate our thoughts, discussion, and actions, so too do great coaches."*

the start of a coach/client session to create a relaxed atmosphere or a tone of calmness before launching into the session.

As I have shared the use of inspiration techniques with other coaches in their sessions, here are some examples of successful approaches used to inspire positive rapport and open dialogue:

- Open the session with a quote
- Listen to music
- Recite poetry
- Infuse humor with a joke
- Listen to a motivational speech
- View and discuss a work of art
- Practice breathing techniques
- Experience aromatherapy

There are a myriad of possibilities. The key is to find the approach that is inspiring to your client. One way to achieve this is by asking the client, "How do you like to celebrate success?" or "Where do you get inspiration?" or "What do you do for relaxation?"

I have used famous quotes as a way to start the conversation. Quotes are a good ice-breaker in expanding client conversation and actively listening for their visual, auditory, or kinesthetic responses. From the coach's perspective, it helps the coach ascertain how the client is feeling or what they may find motivating or interesting. This approach also gives the coach some cues as to what questions to ask and how to ask them. It helps the client consider the possibilities of various forms of expression, particularly when asked, "How do you describe it?"

Consider the example of viewing a work of art as a starting point. Ask the client what he/she sees in the painting or photograph and allow them to express their observations fully. Ask them, "What else do you see?" This form of open creative expression can move clients towards the discovery of multiple opportunities and create awareness of a variety of possibilities in their lives that they were unaware existed.

The art example reminds me of a trip my husband and I took to China six years ago. While in Shanghai, we visited an art gallery where we both were stunned by a picture we saw hanging on the wall. It was a pastoral scene of a couple walking hand-in-hand down a winding road. Their backs were to the viewer so their faces were unseen. The image that we both derived from the scene was that they were about to turn the corner not knowing what awaited them, and they were going to take the journey together. We journeyed to China not expecting to purchase art, and especially not at the price this painting was offered. Yet, we both knew at that moment, we simply had to have this piece! It spoke to us in an unexpectedly profound way. The picture illumined for us exactly where we were at that particular stage of life. We were building a new house, about to embark on another exciting chapter of our lives as we were actively planning to relocate to another part of the country. We were motivated to purchase the picture. We hung it in our new home eighteen months later. It became the focal point around which the entire house was decorated. We even named it. We call it "The Journey." When friends come to visit for the first time, they often remark how much they love the painting of the two of us. The artist didn't paint us. The artist inspired us. We made a connection to the journey in the painting and to the choices we all make in going the distance toward our goal.

UNDERSTANDING YOUR MOTIVATION TO COACH

The coach/client relationship is a partnership in which the coach provides perspective and is a sounding board to the client helping them realize and articulate opportunities that move towards their goal. The coach is the client's strategic partner for focus, accountability and motivation. The client is the leader of the ultimate outcome. They provide the answers to the powerful questions coaches ask. How do you as a coach effectively partner for their motivation? One way is by using tools, techniques, and models that inspire.

"The client is the leader of the ultimate outcome."

Perhaps then, the best way to understand how to coach for motivation is to start with your motivation to coach from the inside-out. As coaches, we are trained to ask powerful questions and asking the question "Why?" is not one of them. We have been trained to avoid asking our clients "Why?" because it puts the client on the defense and could potentially shut them down. As the coach, how well we understand our own motivation to coach is valuable in how we develop rapport with our clients. How is this inside-out approach to thinking, acting, and communicating beneficial to you as a coach?

> *"As the coach, how well we understand our own motivation to coach is valuable in how we develop rapport with our clients."*

Take a moment to examine your introduction. What is your elevator pitch when you introduce yourself to a stranger or prospective client? Take the time to work through your answers to these questions:

Reasons?
- *I believe in making a life changing difference by helping clients grow personally and professionally.*

How?
- *I make a difference by creating awareness, sharing affirmations, and actively listening to clients in regular one-to-one coaching.*

What?
- *I inspire clients to become better leaders, make better decisions, and get better results.*

The next time you introduce yourself to a prospective client, speak from the inside-out with the answers to the questions that you have developed. As you coach your clients on their motivation to do something, encourage them to do the same.

Congratulations! You're on your way to becoming a phenomenal coach.

WHAT'S IN YOUR MOTIVATION TOOLBOX?

How beneficial are inspirational and motivational resources in your coaching practice? What inspirational resources do you use? Clients feel valued when coaches indicate acceptance of their thoughts through active and reflective listening.

> *"Clients feel valued when coaches indicate acceptance of their thoughts through active and reflective listening."*

Earlier, I talked about the use of phenomenal words to affirm, inspire and empower clients. Affirmation statements are a powerful tool to do the same thing.

Affirmations may be a brief three to five word sentences or several pages long. The key in writing meaningful affirmations is to utilize the client's stated goals and aspirations. These goals may range from a very personal lifestyle wish to a career aspiration. Affirmations that are more expansive than one sentence utilize phenomenal words to create positive, empowering statements that support the client's goals. Each paragraph of these more expansive statements is written as one long run-on sentence in a stream-of-consciousness fashion.

One-sentence affirmations are often written in the first person for the client. Clients are encouraged to post them in places where they can be viewed as reminders throughout the day:
- I delight in myself.
- I create value.
- I take care of my heart.

More expansive affirmations are initially written in the second person and read to the client. These statements are infused with a host of phenomenal words. In the following example, the one-sentence affirmation, "I delight in myself" is referenced and phenomenal words *experience, naturally, peace, tranquil, calm, now, realize, create, aware, brilliant, balance*, and *because*, are used:

> "You delight in your experiences and are naturally at peace with yourself because the tranquility and calm that you now realize is of your own creation and gives you a self-awareness resulting in brilliant conversations of balance between you and all those with whom you speak because the buy-in and understanding you so desire in your life you now realize is what you are creating."

What's in a Name?

In today's ever-changing global society, names hold value in many cultures. Celebrities and other notable individuals view their names as brands. In the true marketing sense, a brand is a distinctive name indicating identity. Brands connote a sense of worth in the minds of consumers. A good brand invites prospects to see the brand as the one great solution to their challenge. Strong brands create value.

Qualities of a good brand can be both inspirational and aspirational. Strong brands are credible, motivating, and memorable. They provide a connection that is often emotional for the prospect, which makes them powerful.

In my work as a marketing executive, branding was an essential part of conveying value to consumers in the product and services I developed and promoted. As I worked with people outside of my professional life in community and civic settings, I discovered that the notion of branding has relevance in everyday living.

Just as marketers empower a sense of worth through effective branding, coaches empower clients through the use of affirmation statements. In my work as a coach, I find the use of affirmations with clients to be quite powerful. Written or recorded affirmation statements that coaches prepare for their clients may be referred to any time the client chooses. They are important tools in helping clients move toward their goals. They are positive reminders of the possible outcomes of fulfillment that loom ahead.

> *"Just as marketers empower a sense of worth through effective branding, coaches empower clients through the use of affirmation statements."*

I also discovered that client motivation is augmented when affirmations are coupled with the use of a model I developed and have termed "Phenomenal Branding."

I learned about phenomenal words in my coach training with Cathy Liska at the Center for Coaching Certification. In this training, I was introduced to twenty positive, affirming, and empowering words listed on the left column of the following chart. I have since added other positive words to this list to create a resource bank of words that, when alphabetized; hold some representation of the entire alphabet.

Phenomenal Brands are two or more phenomenal and/or positive words that when used together create an expression that is empowering and inspiring.

PHENOMENAL BRANDING CHART:

Letter	Phenomenal Words	Positive Words
A	Aware	Abundance, Amazing
B	Balance, Because, Brilliant	Beautiful
C	Calm, Clarity, Create	
D		Discover, Discovery, Dynamic
E	Easily, Enlighten, Expand, Experience	
F	Focus	Faith, Flow
G		Generate, Grace, Growing
H		Harmonious, Healing, Honor
I	Imagine	Insightful, Inspirational, Inspiring
J		Journey, Joy, Joyful
K		Kind, Knowledge, Knowing
L		Light, Living, Love, Loving, Luminous
M		Magnificent, Manifest, Motivate
N	Naturally, Now	Nature
O	Opportunity	Open, Outstanding
P	Peaceful	Perceptive, Purposeful
Q		Quality, Questioning,
R	Realize	Reflective, Remarkable

S		Spirit
T	Tantalizing, Tranquil	Truth
U		Understanding, Unique, Unlimited
V	Visualize	Visionary, Vitality
W		Worthwhile, Worthy
X		Xpress
Y		You, Your, Yours
Z		Zest

"Enlighten Clarity," "Brilliant Discovery," and "Luminous Spirit" are all examples of Phenomenal Brands. In the first instance, two phenomenal words are used. In the second, both a phenomenal word and a positive word are used. The third example illustrates the use of two positive words. All are inspirational. All empower. They create a feeling of positive well-being and are uplifting.

HOW TO USE PHENOMENAL BRANDS

Phenomenal Brands may be used a variety of ways. In the spring of 2009, I was asked to speak to the women of my church at our annual Women's Day Sunday morning service. I chose as my topic, "A Woman's W.O.R.T.H." The acronym W.O.R.T.H. represented the words: Walking Obediently and Repentantly Towards Holiness. Admittedly, this was a big, audacious goal! Even then, I was struck with the notion of branding the essence of one's identity in an inspirational way. I discussed the value created by powerful, positive spoken words. We experience joy in hearing ourselves defined in a positive light. That joy is inspiring and motivating. Our positive outlook moves us forward.

I presented a chart, similar to the Phenomenal Branding Chart, that I developed by choosing words (and their forms) found in biblical scripture and next I alphabetized the words. Then I suggested to the congregation they each create a new name for themselves by taking their initials, i.e., the first letter of their first, middle, and last names, and selecting a word from the list I provided that began with the letter of each of their initials. Two-word names without a middle name and hyphenated last names also work with this model. I encouraged them to write out their new "brand names." Their new "brand name" I called their "Spiritual Brand."

> *"The idea is that when we allow these spiritual aspirations to live in us, and act on them, we make manifest our W.O.R.T.H. or value to others."*

In this context, Spiritual Brands are aspirations for a Life in the Spirit. The idea is that when we allow these spiritual aspirations to live in us, and act on them, we make manifest our W.O.R.T.H. or value to others. Ultimately, what we aspire to illumine is the face of God.

SPIRITUAL BRANDING CHART

Write your initials here: ____ ____ ____

Write the Spiritual Brand that corresponds with your initials here:

_____ _____ _____

	Spiritual Brand	*Context*	**Key Verse(s)**
A	Anointed	*Luke 4; Acts 10*	Luke 4: 18-19; Acts 10:38
B	Beauty/Beautiful/Beautifully	*1 Pet 3*	1 Peter 3:4
C	Christian/Christianity	*1 Pet 4*	1 Peter 4:16-17
D	Disciple/Disciple's	*John 8*	John 8:31-32
E	Evangelize/Evangelizes/Evangelist/Evangelizing	*Eph 4*	Ephesians 4:11
F	Faith/Faithful/Faithfully	*Rom 10*	Romans 10:17
G	Good/Goodness	*Gal 5-6*	Galatians 6:10
H	Holy/Holiness	*1 Pet 1*	1 Peter 1:13-16
I	Instrument/Instrumental	*2 Tim. 2*	2 Timothy 2:21
J	Joy/Joyous/Joyful/Joyfully	*Gal 5; 1 Thes 5*	Gal 5:22; 1 This 5:16-18

K	Kind/Kindly/Kindness	*Gal 5; Col 3*	Gal 5:22; Col 3:12
L	Love/Loves/Love's/Loving/Lovingly	*John 13*	John 13:34-35
M	Minister/Ministers/Ministry	*1 Tim. 4*	1 Timothy 4:6
N	Noble/Nobly	*Phil 4*	Philippians 4:8
O	Obey/Obeys/Obedience/Obedient/Obediently	*1 Pet 1*	1 Peter 1:22-23
P	Peace/Peacefully/Peacemaker	*Gal 5; Rom 14*	Gal 5:22; Romans 14:19
Q	Quality/Qualities	*2 Pet 1*	2 Peter 1:14
R	Rejoice/ Rejoicing	*Phil 4*	Philippians 4:5
S	Sincere/Sincerely/Sincerity	*2 Cor 2; James 3*	2 Cor 2:17; James 3:17
T	Truth/Truths/Truthful/Truthfully/Truth-seeker	*Jn 3,14*	John 3:21; John 14:6
U	Unity	*Eph 4*	Ephesians 4:3
V	Virtue/Virtuous	*Col 3*	Colossians 3:12-14
W	Wholehearted/Wholeheartedly/Wholeheartedness	*Eph 6*	Ephesians 6:7

X	Christ (the 1st letter of the Greek form of Christ)	*1 Jn 3; 1 Pet 4*	1 John 3:23; 1 Peter 4:16-17
Y	Yearn/Yearns/Yearning (Longing or Aspiration)	*2 Cor 5*	2 Cor 5:2
Z	Zeal/Zealous/Zealously	*Rom 12*	Romans 12:11

As I closed my speech, I looked out into the congregation and began to speak the Spiritual Brands of several people sitting in the pews. Speaking the brands directly to individuals and hearing the brands articulated proved to be powerful. The feedback I received from sharing this experience was truly enlightening. I learned that this form of expression expanded perspectives, while generating clarity for some, and awareness of purpose and worth for others.

The presentation on "Spiritual Branding" became the forerunner to my development of Phenomenal Branding years later. Phenomenal Brands are used in much the same way as Spiritual Brands. They may be used simply as an aspirational brand name for clients. They are spoken aloud to clients and written for their private reflection.

By way of example, my Phenomenal Brand name is: Enlighten Beautiful Truth. In a one-sentence affirmation, my Phenomenal Brand is used this way: "I enlighten beautiful truth." This one-sentence affirmation is easy to commit to memory. I can post it on the visor of my car or on my bathroom mirror as a gentle reminder of what I aspire to do every day. When a Phenomenal Brand is used in an expansive affirmation statement, it is initially written for the client in the second person: You enlighten beautiful truth. This statement is used as the closing statement to the affirmation. It seals the affirmation in a very powerful way. When the coach gives the affirmation to the client, it is delivered in the first person for the client to use.

In choosing the words to form a Phenomenal Brand, choose words that link specifically to the goals, aspirations, and outcomes expressed by the client. Phenomenal Brands developed in this way achieve the greatest relevance for the client.

As an example, here are some one-sentence affirmations for a hypothetical client, Nancy Denver, based on her articulation of what she wants in the many facets of her life (personal, relationship, financial, career, health, and lifestyle).
- I am experiencing peace and contentment.
- I am easily expressing my desires.
- I am saving for my future.
- I am expressing my creativity.
- I am healthy in mind, body and spirit.
- I am balancing the things I enjoy doing.

Here are several choices for her Phenomenal Brand:
Naturally Discover, Naturally Discovery, Naturally

Dynamic, Now Discover, Now Discovery, Now Dynamic, Nature Discover, Nature Discovery, Nature Dynamic

The two that may best fit together with her stated wants are:
- Naturally Discover
- Naturally Dynamic

I encourage the use of various forms of a positive or phenomenal word in forming Phenomenal Brands to create an aspiration or action brand that makes sense when the words are linked together (*Peacefully Live* in place of *Peace Live*).

I recently shared Phenomenal Branding with a few coaches in a coaching webinar I conducted also entitled "The Phenomenal Coach." Little did I know that it would become a full circle experience for me personally. I was delighted to hear from one of the coaches, months later, thanking me for the inspiration. He incorporated some of the inspiration techniques I discussed into the design of his coaching website. He invited me to view the website. I was struck by his use of Phenomenal Brands throughout as section headers to the various web pages. I was also moved by his choice of photography and background music. The carefully chosen words, music, and visuals evoked a feeling of calm and tranquility. The music selection, in particular, was beautiful and inspired inner reflection and clarity. I was so moved by the music that I downloaded the sheet version that day and began playing the piano again…something that has been a real personal goal of mine for many years. The inspiration was brilliant. Actually, it was phenomenal.

How to use Phenomenal Branding with a Group Affirmation

Phenomenal Branding is affirming individually and also in a group setting. Consider developing an affirmation statement for a group or team of individuals. Recently, I had the experience of developing an affirmation for a group of coaches in a training experience. During the course of our time together, each coach expressed a specific outcome they wanted to achieve. In developing the affirmation statement, I began by articulating their expressed wants in one-sentence affirmations:

- I am bold.
- I am healthy in mind, body, and spirit.
- I am using technology.
- I am balancing risk.
- I am easily innovating.
- I am inspiring others.

I wrote the Group Affirmation statement and read it aloud to the group three times. The first time I read it in the third person, i.e., "We are bold..." The second time I read it in the second person, i.e., "You are bold..." The third time I read the affirmation in the first person, "I am bold ...." I asked the group to close their eyes while listening to all three versions I read aloud.

Here is an example of the group affirmation initially read in the third person: "We are calm and bold now because we easily visualize the balance of risk that is tantalizing with abundant experiences and we enlighten as we easily use technology because it expands our opportunities to grow and imagine brilliant innovations we realize a healthy mind body and a tranquil spirit now aware of a luminous peaceful clarity of focus that naturally motivates us to create and inspire. We Motivate Living and Realize Understanding while Living Balance we Discover Brilliance and Joyfully Motivate Loving Peace. We are Phenomenal Coaches."

The affirmation statement utilizes the individual one-sentence affirmations illustrated earlier, and ends with the affirmation of each individual's Phenomenal Brand.

How does this approach to building rapport, awareness, and affirmation work within the framework of your coaching practice? That is for you to decide. These are just a few of the many tools to expand and discover with your clients as your partnership grows, phenomenally.

Evette Beckett-Tuggle is a Certified Master Coach and a multi-faceted business leader. She is recognized as an excellent presenter and facilitator, and shares her more than 25 years of business leadership in marketing, economic development, and general management through workshops, forums, and spiritual retreats.

Evette has held senior management positions in Citigroup, Avon Products, Tambrands, and Essence Magazine. She served as President and CEO of Carolinas Minority Supplier Development Council and was Executive Director simultaneously in both Economic Development and the Office of Minority Affairs.

Her energy extends to an active commitment to church, civic, and philanthropic service. She is a member of the Harvey B. Gantt Center for African American Arts & Culture, the Foundation for the Carolinas' Robinson Center for Civic Leadership, and the Crown Jewels (NC) Chapter of the Links. She founded IN SPIRITUS Dance Ministry.

Evette holds an MBA degree in Marketing and Finance from Columbia University and a Bachelor of Arts degree in English and Drama from Tufts University. She is the CEO/Founder of Noble Woman Enterprises.

EvetteBeckettTuggle@gmail.com

THE STRUCTURED DISCERNMENT PROCESS
Patricia Hughes

When Amy (not her real name), a principal architect at a successful firm, learned that the founder and long-time Chief Executive Officer would retire in a year, she had a decision to make: be led by someone new, leave the company, or take on the CEO position herself. The decision wasn't immediately clear to her, so she hired a coach to figure out what she wanted to do.

Likewise, Matt (also not his real name), had served for 15 years as an executive director of a non-profit agency. He wondered if it was time to leave the organization, or whether he could whole-heartedly commit for another five to ten years. He hired a coach to figure out what he wanted to do next.

People hire a coach for different reasons. Many years ago, hiring a coach was a way to fix toxic behavior, or as the last step before getting fired. Today, most coaching clients are high-level or high-potential professionals seeking to sharpen their skills and be successful at their jobs. With so many industries in flux, clients are seeking help to navigate the new economy and get promoted. Clients seek coaches so frequently that today, executive coaching has become a billion-dollar industry.

> *"Today, most coaching clients are high-level or high-potential professionals seeking to sharpen their skills and be successful at their jobs."*

Amy and Matt recently sought coaching from Trillium Leadership Consulting in Seattle. They each wanted a sounding board, some help with a transition, and some skill development. Other coaching clients at Trillium recently included a middle school dean who wondered whether she was ready to seek a position as the head of school. Another woman was considering the executive directorship of the non-profit where she was employed. A friend, who quit her advocacy job to accompany her husband to Southeast Asia for two years, wanted to know what to do when she returned to America.

Each of these men and women shared a common question: "What do I want?" This is a question of discernment. Discernment in coaching is a combination of the most popular reasons people seek a coach: to develop potential, work through a transition, and use a sounding board. So, what did these folks decide? How did they get there?

This chapter presents a guided process for getting from not knowing to knowing. The chapter explores what discernment is, and a structured approach to move from a place of confusion, anxiety and worry, to a place of certainty, relief, and joy.

What is Discernment?

The common understanding of discernment is to detect,

distinguish, or discriminate. It is the ability to judge well; to see and understand situations and people clearly and intelligently. Furthermore, a discerning individual is considered to possess a certain wisdom and insight. He or she is able to judge the value and quality of an idea or project, often going beyond mere perception to a deeper level of understanding.

Discernment in coaching is similar. The coach helps a client evaluate so they distinguish between different options, understand the ramifications, and reach a decision. The client may want help thinking through many options, aligning their strengths with opportunities, and feeling confident in his or her decision.

If discernment is good judgment, the opposite is ignorance or stupidity. The antithesis of discernment is to miss the significance of something. These clients shared a fear that if they didn't do some rigorous assessment they would miss an opportunity, become complacent or irrelevant, or perhaps worse, throw themselves in a new direction without preparation and miss the greatness that could have been.

THE STRUCTURED DISCERNMENT PROCESS

The structured discernment process presented here was developed by me after sharing the journey with many clients

who sought to know what they didn't currently know. It is comprised of five steps:
1. Assess Current Reality
2. Assess Strengths
3. Create a Bucket List
4. Engage in Scenario Planning
5. Commit and Communicate

Matt, the executive director, completed these steps in three months. When he came for coaching, he had just spent seven months moving his aging parents into assisted living facilities. He was emotionally, physically, and financially drained. During this time, he estimated he had spent only 20% of his time at work, compared to a normal effort of 120% of his time.

At a retreat with his leadership team, he expressed despair that the situation would not improve for many more months. His team was surprised and panicked by this announcement. Several strategic decisions required Matt's attention and leadership, and the team wanted to know whether they could rely on his leadership moving forward. "We need a leader," they said. "Take three months, then tell us if you are in or out."

Amy, the architect, took nine months to work through the discernment process. She was scheduled to meet with her fellow principal architects in six months to decide who would be the next CEO. "I don't want to be like a deer caught in the headlights and do something rash," Amy said. After six months however, the meeting was postponed due to sickness, which gave Amy three more months. That was enough time for her to make a confident decision.

The structured discernment process begins with understanding how a client makes decisions. Some people make decisions by writing out the pros and cons, attaching a numerical weight to each item on the list, and adding them up. Others make decisions intuitively, based on what feels right. Some people make decisions based on logic and analytics, and others by feelings and emotions.

> *"The structured discernment process begins with understanding how a client makes decisions."*

One way to discover clients' decision-making patterns is to ask about significant decisions they made in the past, and listen to their process for making those decisions. This creates awareness of what worked, what didn't work, and what opened up their knowing. By studying several past decisions a client and coach can usually find a pattern.

For example, Matt realized that most of his decisions were made by reacting to external forces. He compared himself to the ball in a pin-ball machine, where the ball is directed by the levers and obstacles it encounters. Matt's decision making style was responsive rather than strategic. The situation at work called for Matt to be more self-directed and visionary.

Amy described herself as a bull in a china closet, willing to make bold decisions even if feelings got hurt. She wanted to be more compassionate and thoughtful because she had learned that how she led was as important as what she led.

There are other ways to understand how a person makes decisions, such the Myers Briggs Type Indicator® and the Understanding Your Client tool developed by the Center for Coaching Certification. The client and coach can also get input from family, friends, and colleagues about how the client has made decisions in the past. This input helps the client develop awareness for how he or she makes decisions. From here, the client and coach are ready to discuss the current reality.

1. ASSESS CURRENT REALITY

Questions to ask during this phase include: What does the client want to discern? What is currently happening in the situation? What is important about this decision? When will the decision be made? What are the consequences for *not* making the decision? What possible outcomes may result?

"What does the client want to discern?"

In Matt's case, assessing current reality began with adding up the actual hours he was at work over the last three months. Because he thought of his parents often and felt so drained, he believed he was there only 20% of the time, which is what he told his staff. It turned out that he had actually been in the office 66% of the time. He was quite surprised when he did the math, and felt badly that he had scared his staff by informing them incorrectly. Clearly it was important to start telling a different story to reflect reality.

Matt also estimated how much time he planned to dedicate to his parents in the future. He had already spent a lot of time moving his parents from their home to an assisted living facility, and had created financial and health plans for them. With these major tasks out of the way, Matt estimated he planned to attend to his parents about four hours every two weeks in the future. This meant being available at work nearly 95% of the time. The result of this self-assessment astounded Matt. "This is really an eye opener, really encouraging," he said. "I was in the depths of despair when I thought I could only be available 20% of the time. I see now I am coming out of that period."

Amy assessed her current reality by gauging her level of satisfaction with the firm. She acknowledged the current work environment lacked trust, with some outright toxicity and drama between principals. On the other hand, she had good human capital with the staff, she was a thought leader in the design field, and had a strong personal and professional support system that could help her through the transition if she decided to go for the CEO position.

2. ASSESS STRENGTHS

The second step is to assess the individuals' strengths and gifts. There are many tools available to assess strengths. Dependable Strengths is a process where the individual recalls several peak experiences from their past, and then identifies the skills or attributes they used in those situations. These include being artistic, creative, adventurous, or mechanical, as well as being strong at networking, organizing, planning, board relations, budgeting, collaborating, listening, or planning.

The Emotional Quotient Inventory (EQ-i), is another tool to assess strengths. This tool assesses emotional intelligence and includes an action plan for development. Another is the Strengths Finder offered by Gallup, which helps people identify their talents. The Conflict Dynamics Profile administered by the Center for Conflict Dynamics focuses on the strengths and weaknesses in a person's approach to conflict.

Using Dependable Strengths, Matt identified strengths that included relishing a challenge, seeing and seizing opportunities, being adaptive and spontaneous, solving problems, being resourceful, and building strong relationships. He did not score as high when it came to being strategic, which is what the organization sought from him going forward. Matt knew he could rely upon his Dependable Strengths in the future; he was uncertain whether he could make the shift to being more strategic.

Amy catalogued the leadership skills she already possessed that qualified her for the CEO position. These included seeing the big picture, being a visionary, being strategic, and thinking systemically. Skills she wanted to improve included delegation and time management, soliciting ideas from others, and enrolling others in her vision. She also noticed some habits she wanted to downplay, such as dominating the conversation, pushing her ideas through, and not taking time to communicate clearly.

Clients usually identify skills and attributes they currently have as well as some they want to develop. Sometimes the skills to be developed are predictable and at other times are less obvious. The middle school dean, for example, was surprised to realize that a more professional wardrobe was important if she became the Head of School, and that she and her husband would be expected to be comfortable schmoozing with donors and alumni. "He is not going to like that," she said wryly, "but he will definitely like the bigger paycheck."

3. **CREATE A BUCKET LIST**

The term bucket list comes from the term kick the bucket, and is a list of things to do before you die.

Most coaching clients' bucket lists include dreams, goals, and passions which, when reached, will contribute to a successful career and happy life. Some questions to identify bucket list items include: What do you want to do for work? What are your dreams for health, travel, friends, and family? What do you want financially, spiritually, and personally?

This is a key step in the structured discernment process and is a main reason the clients seek help in the first place. Many people already know the answers to these questions and at the same time this knowledge may be hidden or deeply buried. Their dreams may be silenced by the negative voice in the head that challenges their right or ability to be an executive, go back to school, travel, start a business, or take time off. Given the time and space to imagine their bucket list with a coach who is paying attention, and given the belief their dreams are possible, most clients are able to name and claim their dreams and passions. Work-life balance is an important consideration in this step. The question, "How do I want to live?" is just as important a question as, "What do I want to do?"

> *"The question, "How do I want to live?" is just as important a question as, "What do I want to do?""*

One way to help a client gain perspective on their dreams is to measure them against current reality. For example, each of us is a friend, perhaps a parent, and perhaps a spouse or partner. We likely have a career. We may also be a manager, an athlete, student, or community leader. We may be a brother, sister, son or daughter, aunt or uncle. In addition, there are other important aspects to our lives, such as financial health, a spiritual life, or various hobbies. The approach is to examine how a client's life is currently being lived in these areas, and to what degree of satisfaction, then compare that to what he or she wants their life to be like. The gap between the actual and the desired is where goals begin to emerge.

When Amy studied the aspects of her life she acknowledged the time she spent on career was likely to increase due to longer, more intense hours as a CEO, especially in the start-up months. She decided the extra effort was worth it. She planned in more down time each day, and more time each month at her mountain cabin to decompress.

After reviewing his bucket list and work-life balance, Matt realized he hadn't exercised much in recent years due to intense focus at his organization. He was formerly a disciplined runner, and had experienced the mental freedom and physical stamina that running brought to his life. He decided to start running again, knowing it gave him both mental acuity and physical endurance to lead the organization over the next five years.

4. Scenario Planning

The bucket list is a cluster of dreams and desires. Now the client can consider different scenarios. This is where the structured discernment process really gets down to business.

Leaders and organizations use a strategic planning method called scenario planning to make long-term, flexible plans. Scenarios usually combine facts with key driving inputs from the external environment such as political, industrial, social, and financial factors, with permutations of what the future might bring.

After reviewing her strengths and bucket list, Amy developed three scenarios.

- Scenario #1: Stay at the firm without taking a leadership role. She would remain a principal architect and follow a new CEO, accepting whatever situation evolved with her partners. Amy quickly realized this scenario did not include the most important items on her list of dreams, such as growing as a leader, improving her company's market share, collaborating with others, and being a thought leader in the field of architecture.

- Scenario #2: Leave the company and start her own firm. Amy had many contacts and could potentially start her own company. The financial toll would be significant. Plus, she didn't feel done with her current firm. She had invested 15 years developing her client base, the company reputation, and the younger designers, and would feel extremely dissatisfied leaving all that behind right now.

- Scenario # 3: Seek the CEO role. This meant inheriting the office culture and drama. "The worst case is that I simply become very good at managing the dysfunction that is unique to our office," she said. Amy worried the principal architects would not work as a team. She feared their dysfunction would drive them apart, and they would end up acting as separate studios rather than one business. Her heart's desire was to foster strong collaboration with a shared purpose for the business among all the principals and staff.

With this in mind, she developed a list of conditions under which she would take the helm. These included asking the other principals to work more collaboratively, share the marketing and human resource functions more evenly, and meet more frequently to develop office-wide systems such as performance appraisals and employee shares.

Matt likewise determined three scenarios.

- Scenario #1: Leave the organization. When Matt was deeply engaged caring for his parents, he felt the demands on his personal time were so great he would have to leave the organization. After he got his parents settled into the assisted living facility, Matt realized how much time he actually had available. With this fresh perspective, Matt recognized that he very much wanted to stay and lead the organization.

- Scenario #2: Lead the organization by continuing to respond to requests from the community. This is the pin-ball approach in which Matt had previously excelled. This approach resulted in a very diverse set of programs that met community interests and Matt's strengths were particularly suited for this scenario. Matt felt this approach was unwieldy, unfocused, difficult to predict, and did not meet many strategic objectives and opportunities.

- Scenario #3: Lead the organization strategically. The staff and board had envisioned several initiatives which required a more intentional and strategic approach. In one instance, they made promises to the community and failed to deliver. Being strategic would require Matt to change his leadership approach. This scenario was most likely to incorporate many of his bucket list items, such as growing the agency and leaving a legacy.

5. COMMIT AND COMMUNICATE

The scenario planning phase of the structured discernment process leads to a clear decision for the client. This is a triumphant moment! It's important to identify what the client is saying yes to and any conditions around that commitment. This is also the time to label the old story as old, and to let go of telling that story and acting in that way. The client will adopt a new story, communicate the decision to stakeholders, and adopt the persona and actions that will fulfill that story.

> *"The client will adopt a new story, communicate the decision to stakeholders, and adopt the persona and actions that will fulfill that story."*

For example, Matt stopped telling people he was too busy with his parents to be an effective Executive Director. After discerning, Matt chose the third option. He worked out a communication plan that was both enjoyable and immediate: he hosted a happy hour with the leadership team and announced his decision. They were relieved and ready to get to work on the strategic initiatives he outlined.

Matt also created a vision board in his office with sticky notes for each of the strategic goals he wanted to pursue. These kept him focused on his strategic approach.

When Amy met with the other principal architects, three of them, including Amy, were considered for the CEO position. Amy presented her vision, a new organization chart, and her conditions for acceptance. The others were stunned. They did not think she would want the position, and at the same time, they felt she was the best one for the job. The other two withdrew their names and Amy was voted in as CEO.

After a client finally makes a decision, it's time to set and prioritize goals. Be intentional with how many goals to focus on at a time. The good news is that pursuing one goal usually has a ripple effect that satisfies others.

For example, Matt discovered that his runs gave him unstructured time to think, which often led to a strategic idea or solution to a problem. He stopped wearing a watch partly because he was slower than before and largely because he enjoyed the timelessness and freedom offered by running.

Likewise, Amy made goals to improve her delegation skills. In pursuing those goals she simultaneously ended up developing new systems for lead management and mentoring others, two initiatives she had previously had trouble getting off the ground. One goal led organically to the other.

The client creates goals that are measureable and attached to a time frame. This way the client knows whether and when the goal has been met. Lastly, the goals can be translated into a personal or professional mission statement. A mission statement is an inspiring and practical way for the client to state the vision, affirm the core decisions, and lay out the major goals that get them where they want to go.

Conclusion

Amy and Matt are just two of many people who have been helped by a discernment process. Discernment can be a formal approach such as the one described here, with milestones, goals, and tools. Clients benefit from this approach because it is an intentional, rigorous process, and they can trust that their decisions are well thought-out. A simpler type of discernment can simply be a matter of lending a kind, listening ear. This is the approach the friend moving to Southeast Asia preferred. She had inner resources, a long contact list, and two years to figure it out. She wanted a friend to help her think through some options, and then she wanted to be patient and let things emerge. Sometimes, time is the best friend.

The structured discernment process described here has been proven to help clients and it also helps coaches. When someone contacts a coach and says, "I want to figure out what to do!" it can be confusing for the coach to know where to begin. This structured discernment process provides a step-by-step, thorough approach which also honors emergence and the knowledge that grows over time.

A colleague said, "You can't get to a good place in a bad way." The structured discernment process helps guide the client to a good place in a good way, with confidence that important decisions are being made with intention and thoughtfulness.

Patricia Hughes is an enthusiastic leadership development consultant and coach helping individuals, communities, and organizations increase their leadership capacity for 20 years. Pat owns Trillium Leadership Consulting and specializes in custom-designed leadership programs, leadership and executive coaching, and facilitation.

Pat's coaching and consulting clients include executive directors, private school leaders, leadership teams, teachers, community leaders, small business owners, mid-level managers and front-line supervisors. She is the editor of *Developing Women's Leadership Around the Globe*, published with Antioch University.

A Senior Affiliate with the Center for Ethical Leadership in Seattle, Pat co-developed a powerful group learning process known as Gracious Space, and is the author of *Gracious Space: A Practical Guide for Working Better Together* and lead author of *Courageous Collaboration with Gracious Space: From Small Openings to Profound Transformation*.

Pat has an M.A. in Organization Systems Renewal from Antioch University and a B.A. in Economics and International Relations from the University of New Hampshire. She is a certified coach through the Center for Coaching Certification.

www.trilliumleadership.com

Made in the USA
Columbia, SC
25 April 2018